my revision notes

OCR A Level

RELIGIOUS STUDIES
PHILOSOPHY OF RELIGION

Chris Eyre
Julian Waterfield

 HODDER
EDUCATION
AN HACHETTE UK COMPANY

Hachette UK's policy is to use papers that are natural, renewable and recyclable products and made from wood grown in sustainable forests. The logging and manufacturing processes are expected to conform to the environmental regulations of the country of origin.

Orders: please contact Bookpoint Ltd, 130 Park Drive, Milton Park, Abingdon, Oxon OX14 4SE. Telephone: (44) 01235 827720. Fax: (44) 01235 400401. Email education@ bookpoint.co.uk Lines are open from 9 a.m. to 5 p.m., Monday to Saturday, with a 24-hour message answering service. You can also order through our website: www. hoddereducation.co.uk

ISBN: 978 1 5104 1804 2

First published in 2018 by
Hodder Education,
An Hachette UK Company
Carmelite House
50 Victoria Embankment
London EC4Y 0DZ

www.hoddereducation.co.uk

Impression number   10 9 8 7 6 5 4 3

Year   2022 2021 2020 2019

Cover photo © metha1819/Shutterstock.com
Typeset in Integra Software Services Pvt. Ltd.
Printed in Spain by Graphycems

A catalogue record for this title is available from the British Library.

Get the most from this book

Everyone has to decide his or her own revision strategy, but it is essential to review your work, learn it and test your understanding. These Revision Notes will help you to do that in a planned way, topic by topic. Use this book as the cornerstone of your revision and don't hesitate to write in it – personalise your notes and check your progress by ticking off each section as you revise.

Tick to track your progress

Use the revision planner on pages iv–vi to plan your revision, topic by topic. Tick each box when you have:
- revised and understood a topic
- tested yourself
- practised the 'Now test yourself' questions and checked your answers.

You can also keep track of your revision by ticking off each topic heading in the book. You may find it helpful to add your own notes as you work through each topic.

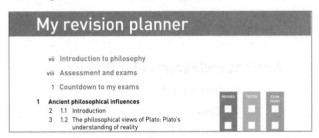

Features to help you succeed

Exam tips and checklists

Expert tips are given throughout the book to help you polish your exam technique in order to maximise your chances in the exam. The exam checklists provide a quick-check bullet list for each topic.

Typical mistakes

The author identifies the typical mistakes candidates make and explains how you can avoid them.

Now test yourself

These short, knowledge-based questions provide the first step in testing your learning. Answers are at the back of the book.

Revision activities

These activities will help you to understand each topic in an interactive way.

Key terms

Clear, concise definitions of essential key words are provided where they first appear.

Key words from the specification are highlighted in bold throughout the book.

Making links

Useful links are provided to other topics within the specification.

Key quotes

Quotes are provided from sources of wisdom or scholars named on the specification to help you understand key concepts.

My revision planner

		REVISED	TESTED	EXAM READY

Introduction to philosophy

What is philosophy of religion?

Philosophy looks at some of the biggest questions about how we see the world around us. Philosophy of religion focuses, of course, on those aspects that are relevant to religious belief – both the foundations of religious belief and also how believers can relate to the world around them.

This component begins by looking at some of the ancient philosophical influences that affect how in the western world we talk about God. It asks what we mean by reality – is what is real to be found in the world around us, or should we look to a non-physical aspect? It then applies this specifically to the body and soul, a fundamental issue because if we have a soul that comes from God, we are defined as beings that were created by God.

The remainder of year one's work looks at whether God exists and how God can be known in the world as well as the biggest argument against the existence of a God that we can worship, the problem of evil.

Year two places all of this in context. We examine the nature of God and make sure that we are clear what we are saying does or does not exist when we speak of God. We then look at length at the language we use to describe God and whether it is valid at all to speak of God in human terms.

Enjoy it!

Bertrand Russell, a significant twentieth-century philosopher, said that we should not be afraid of being 'eccentric in opinion, for every opinion now accepted was once eccentric'. The philosophy course raises some big questions and it is important to challenge your own beliefs as well as others' with new and eccentric ideas. Of course, when you get to the exam, it's important to show that you understand the beliefs on the course, but if you engage individually, then you will really 'own' the material. The examiner will be looking for your understanding of the basics relating to the questions you answer, but will also be looking at analytical skills, which are personal to the writer.

You will get used to writing about philosophical ideas in essay form and you will probably roll your eyes when your teacher sets you yet another essay, but these are opportunities not only to refine your exam technique but to play with ideas and join yourself to the thinking of countless people over history.

If you have a religious faith you might find some of the issues you study challenging, but it is important to engage with them fully, remembering that many significant philosophers are religious too. If you don't have a faith then it's an engaging way to work out how other people think and what inspires and influences them.

What's the point in philosophy?

A philosophy degree at university can open many career doors because of the transferable skills it opens up. Employers in the future will be delighted to receive an application from somebody who can see things from a range of points of view and explore ideas in detail but fairly and comprehensively, as well as being original in thought themselves. Philosophy goes far beyond the philosophy of religion and you could find yourself studying language, existence, ethics, politics, the arts and so much more.

Assessment and exams

How the assessment objectives work depends on whether you are studying Religious Studies for AS- or A-level. If you are doing an AS course then there is no level 6 and the marks are split between AO1 and AO2 evenly. If you are doing an A-level course, then 60% of the marks are for AO2. The difference in weightings does not affect the advice in this book, nor what makes an essay a good essay: you do not have to do anything different at A-level to AS-level, it's just that how good you are at the different skills is given a different number of marks. Equally, don't feel you have to separate out AO1 and AO2 – write a series of great paragraphs and trust the marker to filter things out!

At AS-level, your exam is 1 hour and 15 minutes and you have to do two questions (from a choice of three). At A-level, your exam is 2 hours and you have to do three questions (from a choice of four). *If you are doing the AS-level, you only need Chapters 1–6 of this book; you will need all nine chapters for the full A-level.* Allowing time for settling down and choosing your questions, you basically have 35 minutes at AS-level and not much more at A-level for an essay. That doesn't seem much, but remember that the examiner will be aware of this.

Assessment objective 1: Knowledge and understanding

You will be able to see here that the marks are gained for being able to choose the right information to help you to answer the question. Better essays come from being more precise and knowing a useful range of material which you can explain concisely. The levels of response mark scheme for AO1 is included below.

Level (Mark)	Levels of response: Assessment objective 1 (AO1)
6 (14–16)	An **excellent** demonstration of knowledge and understanding in response to the question: • fully comprehends the demands of, and focuses on, the question throughout • excellent selection of relevant material which is skilfully used • accurate and highly detailed knowledge which demonstrates deep understanding through a complex and nuanced approach to the material used • thorough, accurate and precise use of technical terms and vocabulary in context • extensive range of scholarly views, academic approaches and/or sources of wisdom and authority are used to demonstrate knowledge and understanding
5 (11–13) (AS: 13–15)	A **very good** demonstration of knowledge and understanding in response to the question: • focuses on the precise question throughout • very good selection of relevant material which is used appropriately • accurate, and detailed knowledge which demonstrates very good understanding through either the breadth or depth of material used • accurate and appropriate use of technical terms and subject vocabulary • a very good range of scholarly views, academic approaches, and/or sources of wisdom and authority are used to demonstrate knowledge and understanding
4 (8–10) (AS: 10–12)	A **good** demonstration of knowledge and understanding in response to the question: • addresses the question well • good selection of relevant material, used appropriately on the whole • mostly accurate knowledge which demonstrates good understanding of the material used, which should have reasonable amounts of depth or breadth • mostly accurate and appropriate use of technical terms and subject vocabulary • a good range of scholarly views, academic approaches and/or sources of wisdom and authority are used to demonstrate knowledge and understanding

➜

Level (Mark)	Levels of response: Assessment objective 1 (AO1)
3 (5–7) (AS: 7–9)	A **satisfactory** demonstration of knowledge and understanding in response to the question: • generally addresses the question • mostly sound selection of mostly relevant material • some accurate knowledge which demonstrates sound understanding through the material used, which might however be lacking in depth or breadth • generally appropriate use of technical terms and subject vocabulary • a satisfactory range of scholarly views, academic approaches, and/or sources of wisdom and authority are used to demonstrate knowledge and understanding with only partial success
2 (3–4) (AS: 4–6)	A **basic** demonstration of knowledge and understanding in response to the question: • might address the general topic rather than the question directly • limited selection of partially relevant material • some accurate, but limited, knowledge which demonstrates partial understanding • some accurate, but limited, use of technical terms and appropriate subject vocabulary • a limited range of scholarly views, academic approaches and/or sources of wisdom and authority are used to demonstrate knowledge and understanding with little success
1 (1–2) (AS: 1–3)	A **weak** demonstration of knowledge and understanding in response to the question: • almost completely ignores the question • very little relevant material selected • knowledge very limited, demonstrating little understanding • very little use of technical terms or subject vocabulary • very little or no use of scholarly views, academic approaches and/or sources of wisdom and authority to demonstrate knowledge and understanding
0 (0)	No creditworthy response

Assessment objective 2: Analysis and evaluation

AO2 is about your ability to argue in response to the question. Examiners are making an assessment of your 'extended response' – how well are you arguing? Can you show that you have thought about a range of different approaches to the issue in the question? Are you critical about all the points you offer? Do you develop the arguments you give rather than stating them and moving on? The levels of response mark scheme for AO2 is included below.

Level (Mark)	Levels of response: Assessment objective 2 (AO2)
6 (21–24)	An **excellent** demonstration of analysis and evaluation in response to the question: • excellent, clear and successful argument • confident and insightful critical analysis and detailed evaluation of the issue • views skilfully and clearly stated, coherently developed and justified • answers the question set precisely throughout • thorough, accurate and precise use of technical terms and vocabulary in context • extensive range of scholarly views, academic approaches and sources of wisdom and authority used to support analysis and evaluation *Assessment of extended response: There is an excellent line of reasoning, well-developed and sustained, which is coherent, relevant and logically structured.*

→

Level (Mark)	Levels of response: Assessment objective 2 (AO2)
5 (17–20) (AS: 13–15)	A **very good** demonstration of analysis and evaluation in response to the question: ● clear argument which is mostly successful ● successful and clear analysis and evaluation ● views very well stated, coherently developed and justified ● answers the question set competently ● accurate and appropriate use of technical terms and subject vocabulary ● a very good range of scholarly views, academic approaches and sources of wisdom and authority used to support analysis and evaluation *Assessment of extended response: There is a well-developed and sustained line of reasoning which is coherent, relevant and logically structured.*
4 (13–16) (AS: 10–12)	A **good** demonstration of analysis and evaluation in response to the question: ● argument is generally successful and clear ● generally successful analysis and evaluation ● views well stated, with some development and justification ● answers the question set well ● mostly accurate and appropriate use of technical terms and subject vocabulary ● a good range of scholarly views, academic approaches and sources of wisdom and authority are used to support analysis and evaluation *Assessment of extended response: There is a well-developed line of reasoning which is clear, relevant and logically structured.*
3 (9–12) (AS: 7–9)	A **satisfactory** demonstration of analysis and/evaluation in response to the question: ● some successful argument ● partially successful analysis and evaluation ● views asserted but often not fully justified ● mostly answers the set question ● generally appropriate use of technical terms and subject vocabulary ● a satisfactory range of scholarly views, academic approaches and sources of wisdom and authority are used to support analysis and evaluation with only partial success *Assessment of extended response: There is a line of reasoning presented which is mostly relevant and which has some structure.*
2 (5–8) (AS: 4–6)	A **basic** demonstration of analysis and evaluation in response to the question: ● some argument attempted, not always successful ● little successful analysis and evaluation ● views asserted but with little justification ● only partially answers the question ● some accurate, but limited, use of technical terms and appropriate subject vocabulary ● a limited range of scholarly views, academic approaches and sources of wisdom and authority to support analysis and evaluation with little success *Assessment of extended response: There is a line of reasoning which has some relevance and which is presented with limited structure.*
1 (1–4) (AS: 1–3)	A **weak** demonstration of analysis and evaluation in response to the question: ● very little argument attempted ● very little successful analysis and evaluation ● views asserted with very little justification ● unsuccessful in answering the question ● very little use of technical terms or subject vocabulary ● very little or no use of scholarly views, academic approaches and sources of wisdom and authority to support analysis and evaluation *Assessment of extended response: The information is communicated in a basic/unstructured way.*
0 (0)	No creditworthy response

Countdown to my exams

6–8 weeks to go

- Start by looking at the specification available from **www.ocr.org.uk**. Make sure you know exactly what material you need to revise and the style of the examination. Use the revision planner on pages iv–vi to familiarise yourself with the topics.
- Organise your notes, making sure you have covered everything on the specification. The revision planner will help you group your notes into topics.
- Work out a realistic revision plan that will allow you time for relaxation. Set aside days and times for all the subjects that you need to study, and stick to your timetable.
- Set yourself sensible targets. Break your revision down into focused sessions of around 40 minutes, divided by breaks. These Revision Notes organise the basic facts into short, memorable sections to make revising easier.

REVISED ☐

4–6 weeks to go

- Read through the relevant sections of this book and refer to the exam tips, typical mistakes and key terms. Tick off the topics as you feel confident about them. Highlight those topics you find difficult and look at them again in detail.
- Test your understanding of each topic by working through the 'Now test yourself' questions in the book. Look up the answers in the Answers section on pages 84–86.
- Make a note of any problem areas as you revise, and ask your teacher to go over these in class.
- Look at past papers. They are one of the best ways to revise and practise your exam skills. Write or prepare planned answers to the questions in the exam checklists in the book.
- Try different revision methods. For example, you can make notes using mind maps, spider diagrams or flashcards.
- Track your progress using the revision planner and give yourself a reward when you have achieved your target.

REVISED ☐

One week to go

- Try to fit in at least one more timed practice of an entire past paper and seek feedback from your teacher, comparing your work closely with the mark scheme.
- Check the revision planner to make sure you haven't missed out any topics. Brush up on any areas of difficulty by talking them over with a friend or getting help from your teacher.
- Attend any revision classes put on by your teacher. Remember, he or she is an expert at preparing people for examinations.

REVISED ☐

The day before the examination

- Flick through these Revision Notes for useful reminders – for example, the exam tips, typical mistakes and key terms.
- Check the time and place of your examination.
- Make sure you have everything you need – extra pens and pencils, tissues, a watch, bottled water, sweets.
- Allow some time to relax and have an early night to ensure you are fresh and alert for the examination.

REVISED ☐

My exams

Religious Studies: Philosophy of Religion

Date:...

Time: ....

Location: ....

1 Ancient philosophical influences

1.1 Introduction

Any history of western philosophical thought inevitably starts with ancient Greek philosophy. The three great philosophers of this period around 400–500 years before Jesus were Socrates, Plato and Aristotle. The first of these wrote nothing of his own, but his ideas and character were preserved in the writings of his follower, Plato. Plato became a prolific writer and thinker in his own right and Aristotle in turn was one of his students.

- Plato and Aristotle are different in a number of key respects. Plato relied on reason and believed that the most important aspect of reality lay beyond this world. Aristotle relied on empirical knowledge and believed that the most important thing to do was to gain understanding of this world. They can be categorised as **rationalist** and **empiricist**, respectively.
- What they agree on is the importance of philosophical thought and **reason** as a means of gaining truth. This separates them from Christian thinkers who believe that truth comes through revelation.
- Both thinkers have been influential in shaping the views of Christians and others on various topics.

> **Key words**
>
> **Rationalism** The view that the primary source of knowledge is reason, in the strictest sense, a priori reason
>
> **Empiricism** The idea that observations via our senses lead us to understanding of the world
>
> **Reason** Using logical thought in order to reach conclusions

The specification says

Topic	Content	Key knowledge
Ancient philosophical influences	The philosophical views of Plato, in relation to: ● understanding of reality ● the Forms ● the analogy of the cave	Plato's reliance on reason as opposed to the senses ● the nature of the Forms; hierarchy of the Forms ● details of the analogy, its purpose and relation to the theory of the Forms
	The philosophical views of Aristotle, in relation to: ● understanding of reality ● the four causes ● the Prime Mover	● Aristotle's use of teleology ● material, formal, efficient and final causes ● the nature of Aristotle's Prime Mover and connections between this and the final cause
	Learners should have the opportunity to discuss issues related to the ideas of Plato and Aristotle, including: ● comparison and evaluation of Plato's Form of the Good and Aristotle's Prime Mover ● comparison and evaluation of Plato's reliance on reason (rationalism) and Aristotle's use of the senses (empiricism) in their attempts to make sense of reality.	

> **Making links**
>
> Plato and Aristotle's philosophical method can be contrasted with those for whom faith based on revelation is a better means of reaching truth (see the Developments in Christian Thought book, Chapter 3).

1.2 The philosophical views of Plato: Plato's understanding of reality

REVISED

Plato believed that there was a greater reality beyond the world we experience. He believed that **a priori** reasoning was the key to unlocking this reality. His most famous illustration of these views is his analogy of the cave.

The story of the cave

The analogy of the cave plays a key role in Plato's philosophy. He uses it to sum up his key philosophical ideas. In the story he asks us to imagine that a group of prisoners are chained in an underground cave. They have been there since birth and are chained by their neck and ankles. They can only see the shadows projected on the wall by a fire. They believe that the shadows are all that exists. If one day a prisoner were released and were to venture outside the cave, once his sight adjusted he would realise that it was the outside world that was real and that the cave itself was just a shadow world. If the prisoner were to return and attempt to pass on his new knowledge, Plato argues that he would not be believed and the other prisoners might even threaten to kill him.

> **Key word**
>
> **A priori** Knowledge which is not dependent on experience, can be known 'prior' to experience, e.g. triangles have three sides

> **Typical mistake**
>
> It is important not to spend too much time retelling the story of the cave; marks are awarded for understanding and assessment of the philosophical ideas involved.

The features of the story explained

Plato's story is allegorical and each of the features in the story has a symbolic meaning. This is summarised in the table below.

Aspect of story	The meaning
The prisoners	Ordinary people in our world
The cave	The empirical world that we see and hear around us
The chains	The senses that restrict the way we experience things
The shadows	Our everyday sense experiences
The escapee	The philosopher who is able to access knowledge
The difficult ascent	An illustration that the road to philosophical knowledge is hard
The outside world	The real world, the world of the Forms
The sun	The highest of all the Forms, the Form of the Good
The return to the cave	The philosopher once enlightened feels it is his duty to free and educate the others
The difficulty in adjusting to the darkness	Once a philosopher knows the truth, it is difficult to experience things as the ordinary person does
The persecution given by the other prisoners	Like Socrates, who was executed by the leaders in Athens, the philosopher will be ridiculed and threatened

Going further

Plato's allegory of the cave is in his book *The Republic*. The electronic version is freely available and fairly readable. Section 514–521 gives the story of the cave.

The key messages of the cave

Plato's main overall conclusions can be summarised as follows.

- **Metaphysics. What is real?** Plato's view on metaphysics is that this world is not real and that the real world is an unchanging world of Forms.
- **Epistemology. How do we gain knowledge?** Plato's view is that knowledge is through the mind (a priori) not the senses (**a posteriori**). The senses only provide opinions and shadows.
- **Politics. Who should rule?** The philosopher is the only one who has knowledge and, thus, philosophers should rule. Democracy puts power into the hands of the majority who lack knowledge, the cave dwellers in the story.
- **Ethics. What is good?** It is the philosopher who is able to see and understand the good; they know what goodness is.

Key words

Metaphysics The branch of philosophy dealing with the nature of reality

Epistemology The branch of philosophy concerned with the theory of knowledge

A posteriori Knowledge which is dependent on sense experience, can only be known after sense experience

Now test yourself

TESTED

1 What is represented by the outside world in the story of the cave?
2 Why should the philosophers rule according to Plato?

Assessing Plato's ideas on the cave

Plato's analogy of the cave raises a number of issues.

- It is not clear why it is important for the philosophers to rule if this is only a shadow world.
- Plato may be right to suggest that our senses are not always reliable; however, the information we get through our senses is not unimportant; we need this to survive.
- Plato does not offer proof of the existence of another realm and he is unclear how the two worlds relate to each other.
- He is guilty of elitism. The philosopher is not completely different to the ordinary person. While he may be correct to say there are differences in knowledge, these are differences in degree of knowledge. Having two groups of people – those who know and those who are ignorant – is too simplistic.

In addition to the comments above, it is worth looking at the assessment of Plato's Forms (page 5) and the discussion of Plato and Aristotle's method (page 10) as these are both relevant to the conclusions that Plato tries to argue in the cave analogy.

1.3 Plato's Forms

In the analogy of the cave, Plato has argued that the objects in our world are merely shadows of real objects; the philosopher is able to 'leave the cave' and understand the **Forms** – the true objects – in the real world.

Understanding the Forms

To understand why Plato believes that there are Forms, consider the difference between our world and the mathematical world. In our world, everything is in a process of change: people grow old and die, trees grow and shed leaves, water continually flows. Yet mathematical truths do not change: triangles always have three sides, 2 + 2 will always be 4. Plato believes that there is a similar unchanging truth about every type of object or quality.

For example, if we were to examine lots of different chairs, we would see that despite their differences, there is something that they have in common. Likewise, to use one of Plato's own examples, there may be many beautiful things, and there is one thing that they have in common, this is the Form or idea of beauty.

> **Key point**
>
> Plato states that these ideas which we recognise but can't easily define do actually exist. They are ideas but, according to Plato, are more real than any physical objects. They are invisible and intangible; they are known to the mind.

> **Key words**
>
> **Forms** The name Plato gives to ideal concepts that exist in reality
>
> **Particulars** The name Plato gives to the objects in the empirical world which are merely imperfect copies of the Form

Forms and their Particulars

In contrast to the Form, there are many different objects in our world which may to some extent participate in the Form. These objects, which are imperfect imitations of the Form, are called **Particulars**; they may to a greater or lesser extent have the quality of beauty, to use Plato's example, but none of them is beauty itself.

The world of the Forms (the real world)	The world of Particulars (our world/the cave)
Each Form is one single thing (there is one idea of perfect beauty)	There are many Particulars (many beautiful things)
They are known by the intellect or reason	They are known through empirical senses
They are eternal	They pass in and out of existence
They are immutable (unchanging)	They are constantly changing
They are non-physical	They are physical
They are perfect	They are imperfect

The Form of the Good

The Form of the Good is the ultimate Form according to Plato. Just as a Form is what all the Particulars have in common (all cats share in the Form of the Cat) so too in a sense the 'Good' is what the Forms have in common. The perfection of the Forms comes from the Form of the Good. In the allegory of the cave, the Good is represented by the sun in the outside world. Just as the sun gives light to the real world, so the Form of the Good illuminates the other Forms:

- It is the reason why the Forms are good.
- It enables us to 'see' the Forms.
- It is the ultimate end in itself.

> **Now test yourself**
>
> 3 Which of the Forms is the ultimate Form?
>
> TESTED

1.4 Assessing Plato on the Forms

Plato's arguments for the Forms

- **The one over many argument**. When we observe different Particulars, for example, chairs, cats or beautiful things, we are able to recognise that they are the same sort of thing even if we cannot explain exactly why that is. Even a small child can correctly identify that the new thing in front of her is a cat even though she has never seen one quite like this before. Plato argues that we have an innate ability to recognise the Forms that our souls knew before we were born. Without the Form, it is not possible to explain the sameness. We are able to recognise the 'one' that is over the 'many'.
- **The ideal standard**. The idea of Forms can be used to support a belief in absolute unchanging moral rules. The Form is the ideal standard of a property. While it may not seem important to judge which is the best dog or who is more beautiful (although judges at Crufts and beauty pageants do often agree!), some of the higher Forms, such as goodness and justice, seem too important to be a matter of opinion. The Form of the Good gives us an absolute idea of what goodness really is, it is not a matter of opinion.

> **Making links**
>
> Plato's views on the pre-existence of the soul can be found in Chapter 2, Soul, mind and body.

Arguments against the Forms

Other philosophers reject the Forms for a number of reasons.

- Wittgenstein (1889–1951) rejected the one over many argument with his family resemblance theory. He suggested that there is no 'one over many' but merely a series of overlapping characteristics. Just as members of a family may each resemble other members of the family, but there is no one thing that is specific to the family.
- The Third Man argument also responds to the theory's claim to explain reality. If, as Plato argues, we need the idea of Forms to explain what objects have in common then what is to stop us once we have arrived at the Form asking what the Form and the Particulars have in common and thus requiring a third thing (a third man) to explain this. This process could proceed infinitely and we would never get an explanation of anything.
- Plato's claim that there must be Forms for everything can be carried to absurdity. Must there really be the ideal Form of dirt, hair or even, as Stephen Law argues, 'the Form of the bogey'?
- There is also the problem of new inventions and things that become extinct. Plato's belief in the unchanging nature of the world of the Forms seems to require that the Form of the iPad has always existed and the Form of the T-Rex still exists.
- The Forms do not seem to have a practical value; study of them takes us away from useful scientific study of the world.
- If there are Forms of every possible number, as Plato claimed, then there are an infinite number of Forms.
- The theory of evolution and advances in chemistry mean that we do now have an empirical means of explaining what similar objects or animals have in common.

It can be argued that some of the above criticisms only arise if we take Plato's theories too literally. Plato is ambiguous about whether all objects have Forms. He is primarily concerned with properties such as goodness, justice and beauty.

1.5 Aristotle's understanding of reality

Whereas Plato believed that ultimate reality was beyond this world and could only be grasped by a priori reasoning, his pupil Aristotle took the opposite view. Aristotle's aim is to explain the world around him as this world is the real world. In order to explain the world he uses empirical method.

The four causes

Everything in the world is constantly moving and changing. At birth we are actually a baby but are potentially an adult. You are now actually an A-level student, but you are a potential graduate. In order to explain the movement of all things from potentiality to actuality, Aristotle uses the theory of the four causes.

> **Key quote**
>
> … we must proceed to consider causes, their character and number. Knowledge is the object of our inquiry, and men do not think they know a thing till they have grasped the 'why' of it (which is to grasp its primary cause). So clearly we too must do this as regards both coming to be and passing away and every kind of physical change.
>
> Aristotle, *Physics*, 2.2

> **Key words**
>
> **Material cause** What a substance is made of
>
> **Formal cause** What form or structure does something have, what is it that makes it that type of thing?
>
> **Efficient cause** What brought something about or what made it
>
> **Final cause** The purpose or reason for something
>
> *Telos* Literally 'end' or 'purpose'. The idea that everything has a purpose or aim

1 The first cause is the **material cause**. This is the thing that it is made from, for example, the bronze of a statue. This is the thing that the process of change begins with.
2 Second, there is what Aristotle calls the **formal cause**. This is the structure or form of the finished thing. This is similar to Plato's understanding of the word 'Form' but for Aristotle the form is in the object itself. It is not an idea in another world.
3 Aristotle refers to the **efficient cause** as the 'primary source of the change'. It is the maker of the object, it is the parents of a child or the person giving you the advice that you acted upon. It is this that makes the material transform into its final form.
4 The last and most important of the causes for Aristotle is called the **final cause**. It is the purpose for which something is done or made. In one of Aristotle's own examples, the final cause or *telos* of walking about is to be healthy.

> **Now test yourself**
>
>
> 4 Which of the four causes is the most important as far as Aristotle is concerned? What does this show about his philosophy?

Why the four causes matter

For Aristotle, the four causes illustrate several of his key ideas.
- This world is the real world and the task of philosophers is to explain it.
- The key to knowledge is the empirical method.
- The world and all that is in it has purpose or *telos*.

> **Revision activity**
>
> Take some objects and attempt to explain how the four causes might apply, for example, a statue, a table, a human being.

1.6 Aristotle's Prime Mover

The four causes explain individual changes within the world. Aristotle also believes that the world as a whole needs explaining. This explanation is the Prime Mover.

The characteristics of the Prime Mover

The key to understanding the Prime Mover is perhaps the idea of immutability. Everything in the world is constantly changing; however, the Prime Mover is unchanging. As the Prime Mover is **immutable**, several other things logically follow.

- It is eternal – beginning to exist or ceasing to exist would both constitute a change, therefore the Prime Mover must be eternal.
- The Prime Mover must be perfect. To be perfect means to have complete actuality. Objects in the world have potential, they could become something else. As the Prime Mover does not change, it must be perfect already. Becoming perfect or losing perfection is a change!
- The Prime Mover is also **impassive** – it does not experience emotion. To experience emotion would bring about a change in one's inner state.

The reason why things change in this world is because they are material substances. Aristotle believed that physical substances – all objects made of matter – are subject to change. In order to be immutable, the Prime Mover must be non-physical, an immaterial substance.

The Prime Mover and the world

The Prime Mover causes all the changes that occur. However, the Prime Mover cannot be aware of the world, this would produce changes. The Prime Mover in order to be perfect and unchanging can only think about perfect things. So, logically, it must think about itself and thought. The Prime Mover's perfection moves other things towards him. All things desire the good/perfect and the process of change is a move in the direction of the Prime Mover. One way of thinking about this is the analogy of a cat drawn to a saucer of milk. The milk is unmoved, but attracts the cat. In a sense, the Prime Mover is the final cause of all things.

The Prime Mover and God

Aristotle refers to the Prime Mover as God yet we need to be careful not to confuse what is essentially a **deistic** view of God with the **theistic** view of God offered in Judaism, Christianity and Islam.

> **Key words**
>
> **Immutable** The idea that God does not change
>
> **Impassive** The idea that God does not experience feelings or emotions
>
> **Deism** The idea that God causes or creates the world but is then separate and uninvolved
>
> **Theism** The idea that God both creates and continues to be involved in the world

> **Key quote**
>
> There is a substance which is eternal and unmovable and separate from sensible things. It has been shown that this substance cannot have any magnitude, but is without parts and indivisible ... But it has also been shown that it is impassive and unalterable; for all the other changes are posterior to change of place.
>
> Aristotle, *Metaphysics*, 1073

Aristotle's Prime Mover
Immutable
Impassive
Unaware of the world

Good (but understood in different ways)
Eternal
Perfect
The first cause

Religious view of God
All powerful
All knowing
Interacts with and loves the world

> **Now test yourself**
>
> 5 What are the differences between Aristotle's Prime Mover and religious ideas of God?
>
> TESTED

Assessing Aristotle on causation

- There is an element of common sense in the four causes. Most objects conform to the idea.
- The four causes focus on purpose and this gives us a way of determining whether something is any good or not. We intuitively know that if things don't do the job they were meant to do, then they are not really being the object they were meant to be.
- Aristotle's claim that everything has a purpose is subjective. What the purpose of an object is may depend upon our point of view. A Religious Studies textbook may not have been intended to balance a wonky table but if it does the job who is to say that it couldn't have other purposes?
- Twentieth-century philosophers, known as existentialists, claim that human beings have no purpose. As atheists, they argue that our existence is a matter of chance and that there is no purpose until we freely choose to give ourselves a purpose. However, this purpose is entirely a matter of our choice.

The causes are essentially empirical and as such have the strengths and weaknesses of the empirical method. It is the scientific empirical method that has enabled us to make discoveries about the world, yet, as anyone knows who has attempted to place a pencil into water, our senses do not always give us accurate information. This can be linked to Plato's criticism of the senses in the analogy of the cave.

Assessing Aristotle on the Prime Mover

There are elements of the idea of the Prime Mover that are more logical than the religious idea of God.

- It is more difficult to believe in a God who is perfect if that being is liable to changing emotions. An impassive Prime Mover seems more logical.
- The idea of the Prime Mover avoids the traditional problem of evil. There is no issue about evil and suffering in the world because the obvious question of why doesn't the Prime Mover prevent evil is avoided.

However, there are also advantages of the religious idea.

- It is difficult to understand how a being can be described as perfect yet have no knowledge of the world.
- If the Prime Mover is pure thought but is in some way responsible for everything, then where did matter come from?
- The idea of a 'God' who is not involved is unsatisfactory for religious believers. The Prime Mover is not worthy of worship nor would there be any point in prayer. Although Aristotle sees the Prime Mover as being ultimately good, it is a static and logical goodness rather than the goodness one might experience in a relationship.

Both Aristotle and the religious view of God seem to require that there has to be an explanation of the universe – that the chain of causes must stop somewhere. However, it is just as possible that he is wrong and that the universe is the product of random chance.

Typical mistake

Students can think of the Prime Mover as an efficient cause, a little like pushing over the first domino in a row of dominoes. Yet for Aristotle, the Prime Mover is the ultimate *telos* or final cause drawing all things towards it, a little like a magnet attracting iron.

1.8 Plato versus Aristotle – reason and experience

Use of reason (rationalism) versus use of the senses (empiricism)

The main contrast between Plato and Aristotle lies in their philosophical method.

● Plato favours the use of reason rather than empirical method. Philosophical truths are known a priori without any reliance on the senses. Plato also believes that there are innate ideas; our souls already contain knowledge of the Forms prior to being united to our bodies. The analogy of the cave and the theory of the Forms can be used to illustrate these ideas.

● Aristotle favours the use of the senses over reason. Philosophical truths are acquired via the empirical method using our senses; they are a posteriori truths. Empiricists do not believe in innate ideas; our mind is a *tabula rasa* (blank slate) at birth and it is via experiences that the mind gradually fills with ideas. Aristotle's theory of the four causes helps to illustrate this empirical method.

Assessing Plato

● A priori knowledge gives us certainty but it only seems to give certainty with regard to maths and logic. It does not bring certainty to the things that we experience.

● There are a number of things, such as colour, that are very difficult to know without experience.

● The arguments for and against the Forms (page 5) are also relevant in assessing Plato's rational method.

Assessing Aristotle

● A posteriori knowledge is knowledge of the world around us and is thus more useful than a priori knowledge.

● It seems right to say that we could not have thoughts about most things without the senses.

● The senses can be in error, so empirical method offers probability but not certainty.

● It is hard to understand how we get ideas, such as God or morality, which do not obviously link to the senses.

The Form of the Good versus the Prime Mover

Both Plato's Form of the Good and Aristotle's Prime Mover are the ultimate concepts in their respective philosophical systems. There are a number of similarities and differences.

● Neither the Good nor the Prime Mover is directly or personally involved with the world.

● Both are perfect and necessary beings; they are eternal.

● Both are to some extent responsible for the existence of things in the world, albeit indirectly. They are explanations; the Prime Mover explains change. The Good as a Form is a refuge against the uncertainties of change. It is an attempt to find permanence in a world of change.

● The Prime Mover has consciousness – it thinks about thought and its own nature. The Good is not conscious. It is an idea.

● Both have been influential to the Christian idea of God, though it may or may not be a helpful influence. The Prime Mover has been adapted by Aquinas and others and used as an argument for the existence of God. The Good and the idea of the Forms as perfect and unchanging have also influenced the idea of God.

Exam checklist

- Explain the key ideas presented in Plato's analogy of the cave.
- Assess the conclusions that Plato draws from this analogy.
- Explain Plato's views about the nature of the Forms and which are more important.
- Evaluate Plato's ideas about the Forms and the Good.
- Explain Plato and Aristotle's understanding of reality and the world around them.
- Explain Aristotle's ideas of the four causes.
- Explain Aristotle's understanding of the Prime Mover.
- Assess the views of Aristotle on the four causes and the Prime Mover.
- Critically compare the Form of the Good with Aristotle's Prime Mover.
- Critically compare Plato's reliance on reason with Aristotle's empirical method.

Sample work

One of the potential dangers in writing A-level answers is writing descriptively rather than providing an explanation. For example, in the story of Plato's cave, it is important to focus on the philosophical ideas he conveys. Why he is telling us this story is more important than what he says.

Basic explanation	Better explanation
In the seventh book of his *Republic*, Plato tells the story of several prisoners. They are trapped in a cave and are chained to its floor. Plato says that they have been there from birth and they cannot move their heads. They are constantly facing forwards. There is a fire behind them in the cave and the fire projects shadows onto the cave wall. These shadows are all that the prisoners are aware of. The people who hold them captive hold up puppets and the prisoners have to guess what each of the shadows is.	Plato's analogy of the cave involves prisoners chained to the floor of a cave restricted by the chains on their necks and ankles so that they can only see shadows on the wall. Plato is representing the human condition that ordinary people are trapped by their senses and are unaware of the greater reality beyond what they immediately perceive.

Going further: Descartes versus Hume

In the seventeenth and eighteenth centuries, modern philosophers Rene Descartes (1596–1650) and David Hume (1711–1776) continued the discussion on philosophical method that began with Plato and Aristotle.

- Descartes' Wax Example supports rationalism. He asks us to imagine a piece of beeswax removed from a hive. We could examine its properties: it has shape, colour, is hard and makes a sound when struck. If we left it by the fire and returned to the room later, all those properties would have gone, we would find a puddle. Descartes claims that we would know it is the same wax despite our senses giving us different information.
- Hume claims that all the contents of our mind are impressions (things we experience) and ideas. Our minds are able to manipulate ideas and add these together – we have never seen a unicorn but we have seen horses and horns. If we have no experience of something, we are unable to think of it. People who are blind or deaf from birth can form no idea of colour or sound respectively.

2 Soul, mind and body

2.1 Introduction

REVISED

One famous philosophical thought experiment involves the paradox of Theseus' ship. Imagine that Theseus owns a ship and each year replaces one plank of his ship. Eventually after a long period of time he will have completely replaced his original ship. Suppose an enemy collected each of the discarded planks and put together the original ship. Which would we be referring to when we refer to Theseus' ship? This is similar to the question that philosophers know as the puzzle of personal identity. What is it that makes us the same person despite the changes we go through over time? Plato argues that the key to our identity is the immaterial soul; the body is merely our temporary physical form. In more recent times, Descartes' **substance dualism** has supported the idea that human beings are comprised of two parts – the non-physical mind and the physical body.

Aristotle rejects the ideas of his teacher and suggests that the soul is a way of describing the actions and characteristics of the body. Later **materialism** has supported this view. It rejects the idea that there is a separate soul and believes that the mind can be fully explained in terms of the physical behaviour of the brain.

> **Key words**
>
> **Substance dualism** The idea that there are two aspects to human beings, the physical and the mental. The mental may be identified with the soul
>
> **Materialism** The idea that human beings are made up of physical matter alone

The specification says

Topic	Content	Key knowledge
Soul, mind and body	The philosophical language of soul, mind and body in the thinking of Plato and Aristotle	• Plato's view of the soul as the essential and immaterial part of a human, temporarily united with the body • Aristotle's view of the soul as the form of the body; the way the body behaves and lives; something which cannot be separated from the body
	Metaphysics of consciousness, including: • substance dualism	• the idea that mind and body are distinct substances • Descartes' proposal of material and spiritual substances as a solution to the mind/soul and body problem
	• materialism	• the idea that mind and consciousness can be fully explained by physical or material interactions • the rejection of a soul as a spiritual substance
	Learners should have the opportunity to discuss issues related to ideas about soul, mind and body, including: • materialist critiques of dualism and dualist responses to materialism • whether the concept of 'soul' is best understood metaphorically or as a reality • the idea that any discussion about the mind–body distinction is a category error.	

Now test yourself

TESTED

1 What is the difference between dualism and materialism?

2.2 Plato's view of the soul

REVISED

Plato and opposites

The Greek philosopher Plato (428–348 BCE) provided one of the first examples of a dualist viewpoint. Plato's philosophy often deals in opposites; the Forms and the Particulars, knowledge versus opinion, the philosopher and the non-philosopher. The idea of a dual aspect is particularly important to his ideas about human beings.

The soul and its body

Plato argued that the soul is more important than the body. The body is part of the empirical world and like all objects is subject to change; hence it cannot be a reliable guide to the truth. The body allows us to gain opinions via our senses. The soul, however, enables us to have knowledge.

Our bodies are constantly distracting us from our real purpose: philosophical thought. The soul is the opposite of this. It is immortal and cannot be divided. It is unchanging and most importantly, it is capable of knowledge. This is why Plato very dramatically refers to the soul as being trapped within the body. The relationship between body and soul is not a partnership, it is an imprisonment.

The soul	The body
Unchanging	Changes
Eternal	Temporal
Non-physical	Physical
Possesses knowledge	Gives rise to opinions
Simple	Made up of parts

The make-up of the soul

Plato draws an analogy to describe the inner workings of the soul. He compares it to a charioteer in charge of two horses. One of the horses behaves, but the other does not. Plato explains that there are three aspects present within the soul: the reason, the spirit and appetite/desire. The soul works best when the charioteer or reason is in charge. Unfortunately, the horses often pull in different directions. Our appetites can lead us to things that are not helpful. We also need spirit or will to make us determined to do the right thing. For Plato, a good person is one whose soul is properly balanced with reason in charge.

Soul: past, present and future

In the past, the soul was in the realm of the Forms. The soul has knowledge of the Forms before being pulled to earth by the appetites. In the present, it is incarnated in a body and experiences all the tension of the conflict between body and soul. Plato views the body as a prison and talks of the soul being liberated from it at death. In the future, it will be freed from the body and will be reincarnated into another body or eventually return to the realm of the Forms.

> **Key quote**
>
> The body is the source of endless trouble to us by reason of the mere requirement of food; and is liable also to diseases which overtake and impede us in the search for true being: it fills us full of loves, and lusts and fears, and fancies of all kinds, and endless foolery, and in fact as men say, takes away from us all power of thinking at all.
>
> Plato, *Phaedo*

> **Key quote**
>
> … for if while in company with the body the soul cannot have pure knowledge, one of two things seems to follow – either knowledge is not to be attained at all, or, if at all, after death.
>
> Plato, *Phaedo*

Now test yourself

TESTED

2 What are the differences between the body and the soul according to Plato?

2.3 Aristotle's view of the body and soul

Despite Aristotle being Plato's pupil and living 2000 years before modern science, he does not believe in the idea of the soul as such. Yet Aristotle's views are complex and it is not unusual to find both dualists and materialists claiming his support.

The soul is not a separate substance

Aristotle rejects the substance dualism of Plato. The soul is not something completely extra and different to the body. His reasoning for arriving at this conclusion is based on his understanding of the idea of Form. Aristotle had criticised Plato's Theory of the Forms as unnecessary. Aristotle's definition of a Form is a property that is possessed by something, yet unlike Plato, it is not additional to the object. Bertrand Russell (1872–1970) offers some helpful examples: football could not exist if there were no footballers, likewise redness could not exist as a property if there were no red objects. If we return to the idea of beauty, Plato would argue that beauty exists as an idea even if there were no beautiful things. Aristotle argues that beauty is an idea that we have from observing beauty in beautiful things. Without beautiful things there would be no beauty.

'Soul' as form of the body

- 'Soul' is a description of the essence or properties of the body. It is our personality and abilities. The soul is the form of the body.
- The two cannot be divided; the body is not just a prison for the soul as Plato thinks, but is essential to us. We are body and soul.

Aristotle illustrates the relationship between the body and the soul with his examples of the axe and the eye. He suggests that if the body were an axe, the 'soul' would be its ability to chop. If the body were an eye, the 'soul' would be the ability to see. From both cases, it is clear that there can be no soul present without the body.

> **Key quote**
>
> It indubitably follows that the soul is inseparable from the body.
>
> Aristotle, *De anima*

Aristotle's hierarchy of being

All living things possess soul, according to Aristotle. The human soul is made up of an irrational part and a rational part. The irrational part is made up of a vegetative element and an appetitive element.

- Plants have only the vegetative element, which is essentially the ability to gain nutrition.
- Animals in addition to this also have the appetitive element, which involves movement and desires.
- Human souls, for Aristotle, are different as they also have the ability to reason. This rational part of the soul is what separates human beings from animals.

This categorisation of different creatures is known as the hierarchy of being and has been influential in philosophical and religious thought.

Aristotle and the afterlife

At first glance, it seems obvious that Aristotle does not believe in life after death (see Key quote). However, there is some evidence that he may have believed the ability to reason in some way survives death. If this is the case, it does not mean that our identity survives death, but that the abstract property of reasoning carries on without us. However, this thought is not really developed in any of the writings of Aristotle that have survived.

> **Now test yourself**
>
> 3 How does Aristotle's use of the word 'Form' differ to Plato's?
>
> TESTED

2.4 Descartes and substance dualism

The metaphysics of consciousness

Philosophers have found the phenomenon of consciousness fascinating. It seems that I am aware of my thoughts, feelings, aches and pains in a unique way. While others may tell me what they are feeling or what is on their mind, I cannot know for certain that this is the case nor know that their headache feels the same as mine. The following aspects of consciousness are interesting and require an explanation.

- **Logical privacy**. No one other than me can know my thoughts. I cannot know the thoughts of others.
- **Subjectivity**. My conscious experiences are from a first-person point of view.
- **Qualia**. This is a term used by philosophers to describe how an experience feels to the person who has the experience.
- **Non-spatial**. Although materialists may dispute this, it would seem that our consciousness does not take up physical space.

Modern philosophers (by which we mean the last 400 years!) have attempted to explain the unusual thing that is our conscious mind. In terms of the metaphysics of consciousness, there are two main theories suggested.

1 **Substance dualism**. The view of Descartes and Plato argues that the mind is a non-physical thing that is separate to the body.
2 **Materialism**. The view of Aristotle and others is that the explanation is a physical one and that we are one material substance.

Introducing Rene Descartes

Arguably the most famous defender of the idea of substance dualism is Rene Descartes (1596–1650). Descartes is regarded as the Father of Modern Philosophy in that he introduces a new philosophical method.

Doubting the body and proving the soul

In his first chapter (*Meditation 1*), he explains that it is possible to doubt all things, including whether or not his body is real. His reasoning for this is three-fold.

1 His senses have at times been unreliable. What if they were always unreliable?
2 It is often hard to know the difference between dreaming and being awake.
3 An evil demon – who has nothing better to do than deceive us about everything – could be in charge of the universe.

The final point is a hypothetical one but seems to establish it is perfectly possible to doubt everything, including the existence of the body.

In *Meditation 2*, he realises that there is one thing that it is not possible to doubt; he is certain that he exists. The phrase he uses is 'I think, therefore I am'. This is known as the Cogito from the Latin translation of his words (*cogito ergo sum*). Even if he were wrong about everything, the very act of thinking proves that there is a thinker. Yet this argument only proves the existence of the 'thinking part' of us.

The fact that there is a difference between the mind/soul and the body (one can be proved, one can be doubted) enables Descartes to argue that the existence of the mind is logically independent of the body. For something to be identical with something else, it would have to share all its properties. The fact that there is a difference between mind and body reveals that there are two things not one. This logical principle is known as **Leibniz law**.

Key word

Leibniz law If two objects are identical they have to have exactly the same properties. So if object A and object B don't both have a certain property then they must be different

Differences between mind and body

1 Descartes argues that the Cogito ('I think, therefore I am') enables him to identify the essential nature of the mind and this is that it is a 'thinking thing'. The essence of mind is thought, which is non-physical.

2 The wax argument (see Chapter 1, page 11) enables Descartes to identify the essential nature of physical matter (including the body) and this is that it is extended (occupies space). Remember that this property, extension, is the only thing that remains once the wax has changed.

3 The point is that the mind and body are composed of substances, which have incompatible qualities. The essence of mind is non-physical thought, while the essence of body is extension of physical space. What this means, he argues, is that they cannot be one and the same thing. In a further use of Leibniz law, he argues that whilst a physical thing can be divided into sections or parts, something that has no physical location cannot be divided. Mind, then, is indivisible as well as immaterial.

Typical mistake

Descartes understands the mind and the soul to be the same thing. Do not tie yourself in knots trying to find differences between them!

Now test yourself

TESTED

4 What are Descartes' two arguments for the existence of the soul?
5 What is the Cogito?

Views on the soul, mind and body

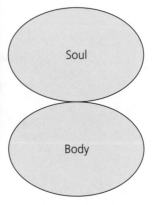

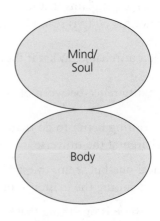

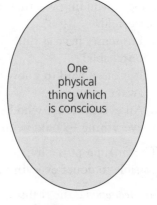

Plato
The soul and body are two separate and opposite things

Aristotle
The body and soul are inseparable. The soul is the Form of the body

Descartes
The mind and body are two separate and distinct substances

Materialism
Our material body, which includes our brain, is the only substance

2.5 Materialism

Modern materialists believe that consciousness can be explained by physical or material interactions. They reject the idea of the soul as a separate substance.

Richard Dawkins (1941–)

Dawkins argues that the idea of a 'soul' is a mythological concept invented by the ancients to explain the mysteries of consciousness. In the same way that 'the gods are angry' may have been an explanation for thunder thousands of years ago, the idea of the soul provided a convenient 'explanation' of the mysteries of personality and consciousness. Yet it is 'not an explanation but an evasion'. Just as our explanation of thunder has been replaced with a scientific one, so too our belief in souls will be replaced.

Dawkins strongly rejects the religious or Platonic idea of the soul but he does accept that it is possible to use the term metaphorically. This is fine as long as we don't believe it refers to an actual thing. He uses the terms Soul 1 and Soul 2 to illustrate the difference.

- **Soul 1**. The traditional idea of a principle of life; a separate thing that contains our personality, the real person. This view is to be rejected.
- **Soul 2**. Defined by the Oxford English Dictionary as 'intellectual or spiritual power. High development of the mental faculties.' This is a meaningful way of speaking provided we are clear that this is **not** a separate thing from the brain.

> **Key quote**
>
> In the sense of Soul One, science has either killed the soul or is in the process of doing so. Probably within the next century, Soul One will finally be killed, and good riddance.
>
> Richard Dawkins, *Is Science Killing the Soul?*, 2001

Gilbert Ryle (1900–1976)

For Gilbert Ryle, our problems stem from thinking about the mind as a 'thing' that is either physical or non-physical. Descartes' dualism, which Ryle calls 'The Dogma of the Ghost in the Machine', is mistaken. It is 'entirely false, not in detail but in principle. It is one big mistake and a mistake of a special kind. It is a category mistake.' There is nothing extra; just human behaviour which can be analysed by science. The mind–body problem comes from thinking about the mind in the wrong way. He illustrates this with his famous example of the university (see page 19).

Susan Blackmore (1951–)

Susan Blackmore spent her early academic life researching psychic phenomena as a result of an out-of-body experience. Over time, she has become more sceptical about such experiences and now rejects the idea that our consciousness is non-physical. While she accepts that consciousness is 'the last great mystery in science', it is the work of neuroscientists that has made the most progress in understanding it. In her book, *The Meme Machine* (1999), she argues that just as evolution can be explained through genes, so too the contents of our minds can be explained by memes, cultural ideas that 'stick' on the pathways of our brain and are to some extent passed down by evolution.

> **Now test yourself**
>
> TESTED
>
> 6 Why does Richard Dawkins reject the idea of the soul?

2.6 Evaluating dualism – the case for the soul

Over the years, dualists have given a number of arguments in favour of the soul.

Plato's arguments for dualism

1 **Innate knowledge**. Plato argues that the soul is required to explain a priori knowledge, particularly innate knowledge. In his dialogue, the *Meno*, Plato shows Socrates questioning an uneducated slave who with gentle encouragement and the right questions is able to come up with Pythagoras' theorem. This and our innate understanding of other Forms seems to suggest a soul that pre-exists the body.

 However, this could be seen as not very convincing. The dialogue itself contains some quite leading questions and the argument relies on an acceptance of the existence of the Forms.

2 **The Linguistic Argument** (sometimes called the user and the used). Plato's argument draws a distinction between how we speak of ourselves and our body. Whereas we say, 'I am happy' or 'I am thinking' in terms of our mental states, we say 'I have a body' in the same way that we might say 'I have a house.' This suggests that we are not our bodies. There is a difference between us (the user) and our bodies (the used).

 However, this is reading too much into our language. I might also say that I have a headache or an idea! It feels as if language has 'gone on holiday' (see Wittgenstein, Chapter 9).

Descartes' arguments for substance dualism

In both of Descartes' arguments given here, he uses the philosophical principle known as Leibniz law. If two objects are identical they have to have exactly the same properties; so if object A and object B don't both have a certain property then they must be different. If Descartes can find a difference between the mind and the body, then it would seem that dualism must be true.

1 **Divisibility**. The body is divisible – it can be separated into parts. The mind is indivisible as it is not possible to separate the 'I' that is conscious into different parts.

 However, some psychologists would dispute the claim that it is not possible to split consciousness. When people suffer from multiple personality disorders they do seem to genuine experience a split in consciousness.

2 **Doubt**. As we saw in Section 2.4 (page 15), it is possible for Descartes to doubt the existence of the body. Yet the Cogito shows it is not possible to doubt the existence of the 'I', the thinking thing. However, one famous counterexample to Descartes is called the 'masked man fallacy'. It may be possible to doubt that my father is the masked robber and impossible to doubt that he is married to my mother, but this does not mean that both cannot be true. Whether we are able to doubt something isn't a property of the thing itself, it is a property of our minds. Just because I think that one thing is uncertain and another thing is certain does not mean that this is the case.

> **Exam tip**
>
> Some of the arguments on these two pages can be inverted. For example, the idea of qualia can be used to support dualism or to criticise the ideas of the materialist.

2.7 Evaluating materialism – the case against the soul

Materialists give a number of arguments to suggest that the soul does not exist and that the mind is really the workings of the physical brain.

1 **Neuroscience**. Neuroscience is the branch of science that studies the brain. Over recent years there has been great progress in understanding the brain. We know which parts of the brain are responsible for language, memory and emotions. Our states of consciousness are affected by brain chemistry; one example being depression, which can be treated by medication that alters the chemistry of the brain. Materialists, such as Dawkins, are very strong in their belief that eventually we will be able to identify all mental processes with the brain and have a complete explanation of consciousness.

   However, dualists refer to the phenomenon of 'qualia'. This is the actual feel of our conscious experiences. They argue that no matter how much knowledge we acquire of brains, this is knowledge from the outside. However, consciousness is a first-person phenomenon and cannot be solved by third-person science.

2 **The problem of interaction**. One key argument for materialists is to point out a possible issue with dualism. How can a non-physical mind or soul interact with a physical body/brain? It would seem that they are completely incompatible substances. One philosopher has explained that this is like asking how the ghost rides the bicycle; its non-physical 'feet' can never apply pressure to physical pedals. Likewise, if our thought that we would like a cup of coffee is a non-physical thing, how does it transmit to our brain and lead to the action of going to the kitchen?

3 **Category error**. Gilbert Ryle argues that belief that there is a separate soul is a **category mistake**. Descartes and other dualists are thinking of the mind in the wrong way. Ryle illustrates this with an example: imagine a foreign visitor to Oxford or Cambridge University. He is shown the colleges, the libraries, the playing fields, museums, accommodation and offices. Suppose he were to say, 'Yes, I have seen all these things but where is the university itself?' This is the same sort of mistake that Descartes makes with the mind. The visitor wrongly assumes that the university is something extra.

4 **Simplicity**. Materialists argue that consciousness being explained by physical and material events in the brain is the simplest explanation. This uses the philosophical principle of **Ockham's Razor** – you should not multiply entities beyond necessity – or in other words you should generally take the simplest explanation. Dualism suggests that there are two aspects of us and that one of these is beyond our ability to empirically investigate it. Materialism suggests we are one substance that can be empirically examined.

> **Key words**
>
> **Category mistake** A problem in philosophy where something is thought and talked about in the wrong way; it belongs to a different category of thing
>
> **Ockham's Razor** The philosophical principle that 'you should not multiply entities beyond necessity'; that it is usually best to take the simplest explanation

Now test yourself

7 What is the problem of interaction?
8 What does Ryle mean by the idea of a category mistake?

2.8 Summary and exam tips

Exam checklist

- Explain Plato's view of the soul.
- Assess the ideas of Plato on the soul.
- Explain Aristotle's view of the soul as the form of the body.
- Assess Aristotle's views on the body and soul.
- Explain substance dualism, including the ideas of Descartes.
- Explain the key ideas of materialism, including metaphorical understandings of the soul and the idea of category errors.
- Evaluate the dualist and materialist positions.

Sample work

Sometimes a question might require you to 'critically compare' ideas – for example, Plato and Aristotle on the soul. This not only means to examine what is similar or different – that is the comparison part. It also requires an evaluation as to which is better – that is what makes it 'critical'.

Basic answer	Better answer
Plato believes that the soul is a separate thing from the body. He argues that the soul exists before birth in the world of the Forms. It is then united with a physical body and returns to the world of the Forms after the body dies. Aristotle believes that the soul is the Form or shape of the body. A human being is one thing and a soul cannot exist without the body. It comes into existence at birth and ceases to exist at death.	Plato believes that the soul is a separate thing from the body. He argues that the soul exists before birth in the world of the Forms. It is then united with a physical body and returns to the world of the Forms after the body dies. Aristotle believes that the soul is the Form or shape of the body. Unlike Plato, the soul is not a separate substance and cannot exist without the body. **For Aristotle, there is no pre-existence of the soul nor does the soul exist after death. It comes into existence at birth and ceases to exist at death.**
Comment: Although the two views are expressed reasonably well, there is no comparison. The views are put side by side and the examiner has to do the work for the candidate.	*Given the difficulties of empirically verifying either the soul or the afterlife, it seems that Aristotle's view of the soul is better suited to our present scientific age than that of Plato.*
	Comment: The section added in bold makes the comparisons explicit. The final section in italics is a critical point regarding which view is better.

Going further: Property dualism

Some modern philosophers, such as Frank Jackson, while thinking that substance dualism and its belief in non-physical souls is naive and old-fashioned, accept that the mind cannot be reduced to just the physical brain. They argue for a position called 'property dualism'. This theory accepts that there is only one substance, the physical brain, but maintains that there are two types of properties: mental and physical. They differ from materialists such as Dawkins as they argue that the mental properties such as having a thought or experiencing a pain cannot be reduced to a specific location in the brain even though they are caused by the brain.

3 Arguments based on observation

3.1 Introduction

REVISED

God's existence or non-existence is, of course, a real sticking point in the philosophy of religion. The next two chapters explore the two different approaches that philosophy has taken to deal with this topic. In this chapter, we look at **a posteriori** arguments and in the next chapter we examine a priori ones and compare the two approaches.

Perhaps the most obvious way to explore the existence of God is to look around ourselves and decide whether what we see (observe) points to God in some way. This approach is known as a posteriori. The Latin phrase is actually relatively new terminology (Aquinas wouldn't have used it), but it is a useful way of referring to knowledge that comes out of observation or experience in some way.

The chapter looks at two famous approaches to a posteriori reasoning about God's existence – the first from the purpose and design of the world (the teleological argument) and the second from the explanation or origin of the universe (the cosmological argument). Finally, we look at common criticisms named on the specification.

Some of the things covered in Chapter 1 will also help you in this topic because Aristotle's approach is a posteriori. Indeed, Aristotle's works inspired Thomas Aquinas, who is a proponent of both the teleological and cosmological arguments. Other forms of a posteriori reasoning do exist, so it's important to remember that these two arguments are not the 'only' arguments; equally, these are not the 'only' versions of the cosmological and teleological arguments out there – and Aquinas was not the first person to suggest them! These are easy ways for anyone reading your essay to question whether you know what you're talking about.

> **Key word**
>
> **A posteriori reasoning**
> Reasoning that uses observation or experience to reach conclusions

> **Exam tip**
>
> The phrase a posteriori is a technical term so could be found in questions on exam papers without any explanation.

> **Now test yourself**
>
> 1 Give a definition of a posteriori reasoning.
> 2 Whose philosophy inspired Aquinas?
>
> TESTED

The specification says

Topic	Content	Key knowledge

Arguments based on observation	● the teleological argument	● details of this argument including reference to:
		  – Aquinas' Fifth Way
		  – Paley

	● the cosmological argument	● details of this argument including reference to: – Aquinas' first three ways
	● challenges to arguments from observation	● details of Hume's criticisms of these arguments for the existence of God from natural religion ● the challenge of evolution
	Learners should have the opportunity to discuss issues related to arguments for the existence of God based on observation, including: ● whether a posteriori or a priori is the more persuasive style of argument ● whether or not teleological arguments can be defended against the challenge of 'chance' ● whether cosmological arguments simply jump to the conclusion of a transcendent creator, without sufficient explanation ● whether or not there are logical fallacies in these arguments that cannot be overcome.	

3.2 Aquinas' teleological argument: The Fifth Way

The **teleological** argument looks at the *purpose* of something and from that he reasons that God must exist. Aquinas (1224–1274) gave five 'ways' of proving God exists and this, his teleological argument, is the fifth of these ways. Taken together they provide five insights into how observation might well point to the existence of God.

The focus for Aquinas is on how we achieve our purpose – it must be due to God. Aquinas, influenced by Aristotle, believed that all things have a purpose (see Chapter 1, Ancient philosophical influences, in particular) but we cannot achieve that purpose without something to make it happen – some sort of guide, which is God.

- Aquinas entitles his argument 'From the Governance of the World'.
- He says that things that lack knowledge (e.g. natural bodies) act for a purpose/end (this is his observation from which he will now reason).
- This acting for an end always leads to the best result.
- This must happen, not by luck but by design (here, design means 'intention' or 'by a deliberate act').
- Anything that lacks knowledge needs something with knowledge to guide it – just like an arrow needs an archer (to get it to its target).
- Therefore, there is an intelligent being that directs all natural things to their end.
- This being is what we call God.

So, for Aquinas, the world is *governed* by God, who is the guiding force that makes things achieve their purpose deliberately. Natural bodies are all things of less intelligence than God.

> **Key word**
>
> **Teleological** To do with something's purpose or goal or end point

> **Key quote**
>
> Therefore some intelligent being exists by whom all natural things are directed to their end; and this being we call God.
>
> Aquinas, *Summa Theologica*

Arguments from analogy

The use by Aquinas of an illustration (that of the archer and his arrow) to make his point is the first example of a number of **analogies** through this chapter. It is important to think about whether it is valid to use an analogy to do complicated philosophy to try to prove (or disprove) the existence of God!

Aquinas' point is that in the same way that the archer guides the arrow to where it is meant to go, God guides natural bodies to where they are meant to go. The natural body needs to get to its purpose, just like the arrow needs to get to its target; the arrow needs an archer and the natural body needs something to direct it – and this is God.

When using an analogy, it is important to consider:
- Am I trying to prove something or just illustrate a point?
- Do the things in the comparison share enough characteristics to make the comparison useful?

So, if A and B have things in common and A is observed to do something, the argument says that B probably does that thing too.

Some argue that arguments from analogy are weak. At best, they can only suggest something probably shares a characteristic. Others say they are useful ways to illustrate a complex argument but are on their own not sufficient. Is it valid to compare the relationship between humans and God to the relationship between an arrow and an archer?

> **Key word**
>
> **Analogy** A comparison between two things in order to help us understand the less familiar thing

> **Now test yourself**
>
> 3 According to Aquinas, humans need God to guide us to our purpose just like an _____ needs an _____ to guide it to its target.
>
> TESTED

3.3 Paley's teleological argument

William Paley (1742–1805) was influenced by the scientific discoveries of his day, such as the realisation that gravity is a controlling force and the planets rotate around the sun. Isaac Newton had shown that a few key rules seem to govern the universe successfully – a bit like a machine.

Regularity

Paley observed that complex objects work with regularity. The seasons of the year happen with order, the planets rotate with order, gravity works with order. This order seems to be the result of the work of a designer who has put this regularity and order into place deliberately.

Purpose

In addition, the way things work seems to have been put together deliberately, with a purpose.
- The eye seemed to Paley to have been constructed deliberately with the purpose to see.
- The wings of a bird operate with such intricacy and with the purpose to aid flight that there seems to be a designer behind them.
- Cells are so intricate that there seems to be purpose behind them.

For Paley, all this pointed to a designer, who is God. Paley used the science of his day to show that on both small and large scales, there is evidence of design; God's creative action is continuous and God will look after humans on a small and a large scale.

The analogy of the watch

In *Natural Theology* (1802), Paley asks his readers to imagine walking in a heath:
- If I were to come across a rock, I could explain its origins referring to natural causes.
- If I were to come across a watch (an old-fashioned pocket-watch), there couldn't be a natural explanation.
- The watch is made up of cogs and springs and so on and this design couldn't have come about by chance – there must be a watchmaker who designed it with the purpose of telling the time.
- The world is even more complex than a watch in how it is put together, so there must be a creator, God.

Paley also said:
- Whether or not we had seen a watch before, it is clearly different to the rock in nature and origin.
- Even if the watch is broken, there is enough design to suggest a watchmaker: he is not commenting on the quality of the design.
- Even if we didn't fully understand the watch, we would still identify design.

Paley's argument uses the understanding of his day about machines to conclude that, by analogy, the world must be a machine with a designer and creator. Paley uses regularity, order, intricacy, purpose and design to make his points.

To what extent is it valid to compare the whole world to a watch, however? Paley was aware of this potential criticism when he pointed out that the watch doesn't need to be fully understood or even working to say that there is a watchmaker, and he also explicitly pointed out that the world is significantly more complicated than a watch.

> **Exam tip**
>
> Be careful how you write about the analogy of the watch. Telling the story is very different from explaining the philosophy and Paley's argument is more than just about the watch.

> **Revision activity**
>
> Summarise the watch analogy and then add another layer to your notes by explaining the philosophy at each stage of the analogy.

> **Now test yourself**
>
> 4 According to Paley, what object is not likely to be seen as designed if you came across it on a heath?
> 5 Why does Paley say it does not matter if the watch is broken?
>
> TESTED

3.4 The cosmological argument: Aquinas' first three ways

Cosmological arguments start with observations about the way the universe works and from these try to explain why the universe exists: 'Why is there something, rather than nothing?' Leibniz in the seventeenth century said that there must be a sufficient (good enough) explanation for the existence of the universe – everything must happen for a reason.

Aquinas gives three versions of the cosmological arguments, starting with three different (although similar) observations: *motion*, *causation* and *contingency*.

The First Way: the unmoved mover

Inspired by Aristotle, Aquinas noticed that the ways in which things move or change (changing state is a form of motion) must mean that something has made that motion take place.

- Everything is both in a state of actuality (how it is) and potentiality (what it might become).
- All things that are moved (the potentiality becomes the new actuality) are moved by something else – things cannot just move themselves.
- The mover is itself moved by something else, which is in turn moved by something else and then something else again.
- This cannot go on to infinity because otherwise there would be no first mover and so nothing would have started moving at all.
- So there must be a first mover.
- This first unmoved mover is what everyone understands to be God.

The Second Way: the uncaused causer

Using very similar logic, the Second Way talks about how everything we observe (an effect) is caused by something else. Using Aristotle's idea of an 'efficient cause', Aquinas is talking about makers of objects (or situations).

- Nothing can be its own efficient cause because it cannot have existed before itself.
- Things that are causes must themselves be caused, otherwise the effect would be taken away.
- We cannot go back to infinity because that would mean there was no first cause of everything and so all later effects and causes wouldn't have happened.
- Therefore, there must be a special case, a first efficient cause that is not itself caused.
- This first uncaused causer is what everyone understands to be God.

> **Making links**
>
> Aquinas uses much of Aristotle's language, covered in Chapter 1.

The Third Way: contingency and necessity

Aquinas' point here is that everything in the universe is contingent – it relies on something to have brought it into existence and also things to let it continue to exist.

- In nature, there are things that are possible 'to be' and 'not to be' (**contingent beings**).
- These things could not always have existed because they must have not existed at some point because they rely on something for their existence.

> **Key word**
>
> **Contingent being** Something that relies on something else for its existence; it is possible that it does or does not exist

- If we trace this back, then we get to a point where nothing existed, but then nothing would have begun to exist as nothing can come from nothing.
- Therefore, there must be a type of being that is not contingent – a **necessary being**.
- Perhaps necessary beings could have their necessity come from another being.
- You cannot go back infinitely with necessary beings being given their necessity by other necessary beings.
- Therefore, there must be a being that has of itself its own necessity (its existence can be explained only by itself) which causes other beings.
- This is what people call God.

Key word

Necessary being
Something that does not rely on anything else for its existence

Now test yourself

TESTED

6 In the correct order, what do Aquinas' first three ways argue from?
7 How does each of the three ways end?

3.5 Hume's challenges to these arguments from observation

REVISED

David Hume's (1711–1776) writings criticise both the teleological and cosmological arguments. Underpinning both is the idea that we cannot meaningfully speak of the design of the world or the creation of the universe because we do not have sufficient experience of either to draw conclusions – the situation and discussion are too unique. He also felt that arguments such as these can only ever say that the conclusion (that God exists) is *probable* because they work on the general evidence we have now and not all possible evidence in the future: for example, we might discover something that does not have a cause.

Criticisms of the teleological argument

Hume's criticisms of the teleological argument actually predate Paley. Paley probably knew of them but rejected them.

First, Hume challenged analogies as a way of argument.
- It is not necessarily true that the world is like a watch.
- It might be true that a watch looks as if it is designed, but it is harder to say that the world has these characteristics. Hume therefore is rejecting the idea that the analogy is suitable.
- In fact, the world could be said to be more like a vegetable that has characteristics of intricacy (a complex natural object), rather than a machine like a watch.

Key quote

The world plainly resembles more an animal or vegetable than it does a watch.
David Hume, *Dialogues Concerning Natural Religion*

Hume used the *Epicurean hypothesis* from about the year 200 BCE, which said that, given an infinite amount of time, all the particles in the universe would be able to combine in every possible combination. Eventually, a stable environment would be created and that could be the world in which we live. Thus, randomness explains the universe, not a designer. The teleological argument does not prove, according to Hume, that the only way in which the world could be as it is comes from God.

Finally, Hume makes some points about the nature of the God who is supposedly proven. Hume objects to the idea that by looking at the effects in the world we can make inferences about the cause – i.e. God. This is the methodology used by Aquinas in his Five Ways.

- Our world is finite and imperfect; why should God be infinite and perfect – why couldn't God be finite and/or imperfect, too?
- Hume uses the example of a pair of scales where one side is hidden: just because we know one side of the scales is heavier than the other, we don't know the exact weight of the other side.
- In the same way, just because we might see evidence of a designer, we do not know anything about the nature of the designer.
- The designer could have created this world through a series of trial and error experiments (just like a watchmaker would, in fact).
- The world could even be the first attempt of an 'infant deity' who then abandoned the world.
- Hume uses the example of a shipbuilder who makes a wonderful ship, but when we meet him turns out to be a 'stupid mechanic' who has imitated others and copied an art-form that has been through many failed attempts.
- There could be a number of designers – after all, a ship or house is created by a number of people; why should there only be one God?
- The designer could be immoral (after all, the creator(s) of a perfect ship aren't necessarily perfect people! Just because a watch is perfect, it doesn't mean the watchmaker is a good person).

Criticisms of the cosmological argument

Hume questioned whether it is possible to make the jump from what Aquinas observed and the God that Christians believe in. The effect cannot immediately point towards a particular cause. For example, when you get the grade that you want in your RS exam this summer, will it come from this book, your teacher or your hard work? Hume said that causation is a psychological concept and we cannot make links between cause and effect that is beyond our experience. Equally, he said that it is not necessary to suppose that everything has a cause at all, which rejects the whole approach of Aquinas.

Hume argued that we cannot make the jump from the idea that just because everything in the universe has a cause or reason to exist then the entire universe must have a cause or reason to exist (this is called the *Fallacy of Composition* and is discussed further below). He said that just because you can explain the cause of each of a collection of 20 particles of matter, it does not mean that you can explain the cause of the group of the particles.

In the context of Aquinas' Third Way, Hume said that it is illogical to suppose that there is any being whose nature requires a contradiction: he does not think there can be a being that cannot not exist because something that exists (by definition) could not exist. Equally, why does it have to be God that is necessary: why can't the universe be necessary?

Examining Hume

- Just because we cannot fully understand God, why should the logic of the arguments be dismissed?
- It is reasonable to look for total explanations of all events – so why not look for a reason for all 20 particles being grouped together?
- Modern science suggests that there is a definite beginning to the universe.

> **Key quote**
>
> By sharing the work among several, we may so much further limit the attributes of each, and get rid of that extensive power and knowledge, which must be supposed in one deity.
>
> Hume, *Dialogues Concerning Natural Religion*

> **Revision activity**
>
> Match each of Hume's points across the two arguments to the stages of Aquinas' and Paley's arguments.

> **Exam tip**
>
> It is important to be able to judge how effective the criticisms raised by Hume are.

- We need faith to make the final leap to understanding God.
- A vegetable only grows because the laws of biology work — where do these laws come from?
- Just because we have no experience of something, it does not mean that our current understanding cannot explain it.
- God does not have to share all the same characteristics as a human designer; for example, God does not have a body.
- The creation of the world/universe is a unique event; why shouldn't there be a special case, such as God, to explain it?

Now test yourself

TESTED ☐

8 What does Hume say that we know about shipbuilders that might make Paley's argument less successful?

Revision activity

Match the criticisms made of Hume's views with Hume's own points. Some could be used more than once. Which could be used in an essay on the cosmological argument, which on the teleological argument and which could be used for both?

3.6 The challenge of evolution

REVISED ☐

Evolution challenges the teleological argument as it presents an alternative explanation as to how the world could exist as it does now; there does not seem to be the need for a designer if evolution is accepted. However, many religious believers feel that evolution can work alongside belief in God because they see it as a tool that God used to make things as they are — it is another example of a simple law that can be seen in the world.

Charles Darwin (1809–1882) wrote *The Origin of Species,* which has defined evolutionary thinking ever since. Darwin's Theory of Evolution was evolution by natural selection — things exist as they are because of natural methods, selecting what will survive and what will not; some suggest there seems to be no space for God in this approach. Twentieth-century discoveries about genetics have only supported his underlying principles.

Typical mistake

It is important to remember that evolution is a challenge to the teleological argument more than it is a challenge to the cosmological argument.

Exam tip

It is important to remember that Paley was writing before evolution had been written about and so do not dismiss Paley without fair argument.

Aspect of evolution	Explanation	How it challenges the teleological argument
Inheritance and reproduction	Species reproduce and pass on their genes to the next generation	This places the emphasis not on the designer God, but on what is going on in the world
Mutation	As genes are passed on mutations occur in subsequent generations. These mutations change the characteristics of the species	Changes in different species therefore do not happen because of a designer but because of naturally occurring mutations (chance)
Survival of the fittest	When new characteristics emerge out of mutations, there will be two different types of one species around at one time. Those that are 'fittest' (most able) to survive will be the ones that do well and will be the ones that will therefore reproduce and so their characteristics will be passed on to the next generation	The teleological argument claims that a designer is what effects change. The survival of the fittest says that it is nature competing against nature for survival that is what makes the change. Therefore, brutal nature is responsible for how we see the world around us, not a designer

→

Aspect of evolution	Explanation	How it challenges the teleological argument
Adaptation	The fittest species will be those that are most suitable for the environment. As the environment changes, the species eventually adapt to fit it; for example, the shape of a bird's beak might change due to mutation but a new beak shape, in turning out to be the most suitable for the available food, becomes the dominant shape; thus the species adapts	This removes the guiding nature of a God who is intricately involved with his creation. Paley's fascination with birds' wings, for example, might be now explained by the need for an early form of bird to be able to fly in order to escape predators
Extinction	Nature allows species to go extinct – such as the dinosaurs	It is difficult to understand why the God of the teleological argument allows such waste of species or would design fallible ones
Development over time	Evolution takes place over incredibly long periods of time	The designer seems to design a species 'all at once'
Chance and randomness	Underpinning all of the idea of evolution is that everything happens by chance. Mutation is entirely random	The design argument rejects any sense of chance; the guiding hand of God is the controlling force

Key quote

In the case of living machinery, the 'designer' is unconscious natural selection, the blind watchmaker.

Richard Dawkins, a modern evolutionary scientist, *The Blind Watchmaker*

Teleological arguments have largely not continued in modern times; however, the anthropic principle suggests that there is too much that has gone right in the world in leading to the existence of humankind for it to have come about by chance. The aesthetic principle suggests that the ability to recognise beauty is not something that would have come about by evolution (because there is no evolutionary advantage to it) and so must suggest a divine creator.

The medieval principle of preferring the simplest option when there is more than one possible explanation (Ockham's Razor) has led some thinkers to suggest that a designer God is the easiest solution to how things have come about. Some fundamentalist Christian groups think that there are organisms that do not conform to the processes of natural selection and so there must be an intelligent designer behind the world. However, given the size of the universe it is difficult to see how our earth can be anything other than the lucky planet.

Now test yourself

TESTED

9 What is the underlying principle of Darwin's Theory of Evolution?

3.7 Logical fallacies

A **logical fallacy** is an error in logic. Those who criticise the arguments for the existence of God have often pointed towards errors in their logic that mean the arguments collapse. Many of the points raised by Hume (see Section 3.5) are accusations of logical fallacies; the example of the 20 particles is a famous one: the Fallacy of Composition, which says that it is an error to look for an explanation of the whole composition of a group, as well as the individual explanations for the members of the group. Some other logical fallacies that arise out of these arguments are below.

- The *assumption* that all things are moved or have a cause or are contingent or have a purpose can be argued to be a logical fallacy because it is just that – an assumption.
  However, it does correspond with what we observe.
- *Infinite regression*: Aquinas maintains that things cannot go back to infinity. Arguably, things can go back to infinity, such as numbers on a number line going back −1, −2, −3 and so on.
  However, this still does not answer the fundamental question about why there is anything in the first place.
- The *jump to a transcendent creator*: we have seen that Hume does not accept that we can move from the observations in the world to the idea of a creator who is the God of religious faith. The conclusions of each of Aquinas' ways seem to move from a very narrow observation to a declaration that the uncaused causer (or mover or necessary being) is the Christian God. It could be argued that this is an error in logic because it is a jump too far.
  However, some might say that all Aquinas is trying to do is to point towards an aspect of God and he is not trying to prove all of God's attributes in such a short part of his work.
- The cosmological argument suggests that there must be a *special case* who is an unmoved mover, uncaused cause or necessary being. This assumption could be a logical fallacy because it is not clear why God has to be the special case. There is nothing like the universe in existence, so why can the universe not be the special case?
  However, the universe is still a 'thing', made up of matter. This point may not fully explain where the matter comes from.
- Paley's view that *regularity and order* must come from somewhere might also be a jump in logic because the regularity could come from chance or the way things have always been (e.g. gravity).
  However, it is important to consider this alongside intricacy and design – the other aspects of his argument.

It is, of course, also a fallacy to say that just because the arguments don't fully explain the existence of the God of religious faith, it means that God cannot exist. One question often asked is whether the theist or the atheist should be the one to be forced to prove their viewpoints. Hume himself was not able to prove the non-existence of God and so could be said to have been an agnostic, not an atheist.

> **Key word**
>
> **Logical fallacy** An error in logic

> **Exam tip**
>
> It is important to be able to challenge every point you make. Good analysis comes from not leaving a point standing alone without engagement.

Now test yourself

TESTED

10 What is a logical fallacy?

3.8 Summary and exam tips

> **Exam checklist**
> - Explain Aquinas' Fifth Way.
> - Explain Paley's teleological argument.
> - Compare Aquinas' first three ways.
> - Explain how Hume criticises the arguments.
> - Explain how evolution challenges belief.
> - Evaluate the positions of Aquinas, Paley and Hume.
> - Evaluate the possible logical fallacies in the arguments.
> - Analyse whether the cosmological argument jumps to the conclusion of a transcendent creator.
> - Analyse whether chance is a sufficient explanation for the existence of the world as it is.

Exam tip

If you are set an essay asking you to explain the weaknesses or criticisms of an argument, it is important not spend too much time writing out both sides of the arguments when you don't have to.

Sample work

This example imagines an essay on the criticisms of the cosmological argument.

First attempt	Improvement
Aquinas' first way says that there is an unmoved mover. Aquinas said that all things are in a state of motion and when something is moving it must have been moved by something else. This could not have gone back to infinity and so there must be an unmoved mover who is a special case who is God. There are a number of assumptions in this argument. First, Aquinas assumes that all things are in a state of motion, which is not necessarily the case. He also assumes that things cannot go back to infinity. Finally, he assumes that the unmoved mover is the Christian God.	Aquinas' assumption that all things are in motion starts off his first way. Hume said that we cannot speak about things of which we have no experience and Aquinas seems to be doing this. Equally, Aquinas assumes that infinite regression is not possible when he says that there must be a first mover, but our experience even of numbers shows that it is possible to count backwards to minus infinity. Another key assumption in the first way is that the unmoved mover is the Christian God, which seems to be a jump in the logic when all he might possibly have proven is some sort of deist God.

Going further: The Big Bang

Modern cosmology generally says that the universe was created about 13.7 billion years ago by the Big Bang. All of the universe was contained in a bubble which was tinier, hotter and denser than we can imagine. At this point, the laws of nature were not as we know them. About 300,000 years after the Big Bang, the universe had cooled enough for atoms to form and their collision created the shape of the universe as we know it.

This simple explanation might explain how the universe came to be, but many religious believers are happy to accept the theory as true alongside their own beliefs. For them, the Big Bang still does not fully answer the question of how matter came to exist, nor of why the expansion started. Even recent discoveries of the Higgs-Boson particle that is self-causing do not explain why the particle was here in the first place. Many theists are happy, as with evolution, to see the Big Bang as a tool that God used to create a simple universe with set laws of nature. The cosmological argument in recent years has focused much more on Aquinas' Third Way and the thinking of Leibniz in order to focus the debate not on causation and process but on an explanation for why things are as they are — why there is something, rather than nothing.

4 Arguments based on reason

4.1 Introduction

The **ontological** argument tries to prove that God exists based on who God is.

- It is ontological because it deals with the nature of being.
- It is **a priori** because it uses reasoning that comes prior to (before) experience – it uses theoretical and analytical (logical) deduction to try to prove the existence of God.
- It is a deductive argument because it aims to prove without question the existence of God (unlike the arguments in the previous chapter that merely point to the existence of God).
- It works from definitions outwards. Ultimately it is trying to say that if you understand the definition of God, then you understand God exists.

There are a number of different types of ontological arguments but the most famous is that from Anselm, whom we study on this specification. Gaunilo criticises Anselm directly as a contemporary and Kant criticises the general approach to the argument. By asking whether the ontological argument works, we are really asking whether this whole style of arguing works or whether the a posteriori approach in the last chapter is better.

Anselm lived from 1033 to 1109 as a monk in France, becoming Archbishop of Canterbury for the last part of his life. As a monk, he promoted a life of contemplation and prayer; the book in which we find the ontological argument is really a prayer addressed to God. It is interesting to consider whether Anselm ever meant for his prayer to become a major part of philosophical study.

> **Key words**
>
> **Ontological** The study of being
>
> **A priori reasoning** Reasoning that uses analytical deduction

The specification says

Topic	Content	Key knowledge
Arguments based on reason	The ontological argument	Details of this argument including reference to: • Anselm • Gaunilo's criticisms • Kant's criticisms
	Learners should have the opportunity to discuss issues related to arguments for the existence of God based on reason, including: • whether a posteriori or a priori is the more persuasive style of argument • whether or not existence can be treated as a predicate • whether or not the ontological argument justifies belief • whether or not there are logical fallacies in this argument that cannot be overcome.	

Now test yourself

TESTED

1 Give a definition of a priori reasoning.
2 What does 'ontology' mean?

4.2 Anselm's ontological argument

In Anselm's work *Proslogion*, he grapples with the nature of God from a number of different aspects. The work is 26 chapters long, but it is Chapters 2 and 3 that contain the ontological argument. Each chapter has a different version of the argument, which we know as formulations of the argument.

First formulation

The starting point for Anselm is the fool of the Psalms. This is the word that the Psalmist uses to describe atheists. Anselm's point is that atheists know what they are rejecting – they understand God because they have to understand God to say he doesn't exist. Therefore atheists have a common understanding with theists of God in their minds.

Anselm's next point is about a painter. A painter imagines their painting and so it exists in his or her mind. Once the painting is painted it exists both in the painter's understanding and in reality. So, Anselm separates two different types of existence – existence in the mind and existence in reality.

> **Key quote**
>
> The fool says in his heart, 'There is no God'.
>
> *Psalm* 14:1

The argument goes on:
- The definition of God is that which nothing greater can be thought of – God is the greatest possible being.
- The atheist understands this as much as the theist.
- Therefore, God exists in everyone's mind.
- But the definition of God is that he is the greatest possible being.
- It is greater to exist in reality than just in the mind (the painting that exists in reality is fully understood only once it is completed).
- So, because everyone (atheist and theist) understands who God is he can't just exist in the mind alone because then there would be a greater being that exists (and God is the greatest!) – and that's a contradiction.
- So, God must exist both in the mind and in reality, which means that God exists.

> **Exam tip**
>
> Make sure you treat the two aspects of the argument separately and distinctly in essays.

Second formulation

In this version, Anselm talks about beings that one can imagine not existing (*contingent* beings) and beings that cannot not exist (*necessary* beings). Necessary beings are obviously better than contingent beings. So, if God were a contingent being then he wouldn't be the greatest possible being – which means that God must be a necessary being. If God is a necessary being then God cannot not exist – which means God exists.

Anselm finishes this section like this:

> So truly, therefore, do you exist, O Lord, my God, that you cannot be conceived not to exist; and rightly. For, if a mind could conceive of a being better than you, the creature would rise above the Creator; and this is most absurd. And, indeed, whatever else there is, except you alone, can be conceived not to exist. To you alone, therefore, it belongs to exist more truly than all other beings, and hence in a higher degree than all others. For, whatever else exists does not exist so truly, and hence in a less degree it belongs to it to exist. Why, then, has the fool said in his heart, there is no God, since it is so evident, to a rational mind, that you do exist in the highest degree of all? Why, except that he is dull and a fool?

Anselm, *Proslogion*, Chapter 3

> **Revision activity**
>
> Use the quotation from Anselm to explore his thinking. Underline phrases and/or words and write a commentary on each part of it, drawing from the information in this chapter.

> **Now test yourself**
>
> 3 How does Anselm define God?
> 4 According to Anselm, what is greater than existing in the mind alone?
>
> TESTED

4.3 Gaunilo versus Anselm

Gaunilo was another monk who lived at the same time as Anselm. Gaunilo believed in God, but questioned Anselm's approach. He wrote *On Behalf of the Fool* to show that understanding the definition of God does not necessarily mean God exists.

The perfect island

Gaunilo's most famous approach was to use Anselm's logic in a different context:

- He says imagine the greatest conceivable, but lost, island somewhere in the ocean. It has all 'riches and delicacies' – more so than any other island.
- If you were told about that island you would be able to imagine it – it would exist in your mind.
- Suppose you were then told that there could be no doubt that this island exists because logically it must be so as it is more excellent to exist in reality than just in the mind.
- You would not feel that anyone had proven anything to you because nobody had shown you that its existence was there in the first place.

Thus, Gaunilo suggests that the internal logic that Anselm had used was equally false.

Gaunilo's other points

- We have plenty of unreal objects in our minds – this is perfectly usual.
- We may even believe something unreal that someone tells us, but this still does not make it real – this is like gossip – we might believe gossip, but this does not make it true.
- The analogy of the painter does not work because there is a real difference between the initial idea and the final product.
- We do not necessarily all have a common understanding of God: a being greater than all other beings might be different for different people.
- You can never fully understand something from description alone: different people conjure different pictures in their minds when the same words are spoken.
- You cannot define something into existence.
- We are fully aware of our own existence but can also think of our non-existence. Why should it not be the same with God: we can imagine God's non-existence as much as we can imagine God's existence.

Anselm's reply

Anselm replied to Gaunilo's points by reaffirming his initial definition of God as being the only being that cannot not exist. He said that the moment you decide that there could be a being that which nothing greater can be thought of, you have placed it in your mind and this is what God is. It becomes a contradiction to say that there is a greatest possible being and that this might not exist. Anselm's point is that God is a special case.

Anselm accuses Gaunilo of misplacing his logic. Anselm was not talking about any object when he made his points but of God, a necessary being, who is the greatest possible being; the island is a contingent thing, unlike God.

Anselm defends his painter analogy by saying that it shows the coherence of his logic. He is not saying the painter and painting *are* God!

Anselm's final point is that in other matters we say the best possible version of those matters are things we attribute to God – for example, when thinking about good, we attribute perfect goodness to God. He says, 'Hence, the being than which a greater is inconceivable must be whatever should be attributed to the divine essence' (*In Reply to Gaunilo*, 10).

> **Revision activity**
>
> Make a flow diagram of Anselm's arguments and to the right, write down Gaunilo's refutations.

> **Typical mistake**
>
> Be careful not to think that Anselm wrote the two versions of his argument at different times – they are different chapters of *Proslogion*.

> **Now test yourself**
>
> 5 What does Anselm say about God that makes him reject Gaunilo's criticisms?
>
> TESTED

4.4 Kant's criticisms

Immanuel Kant (1724–1804) criticised the general approach of ontological arguments, responding to more contemporary versions of the argument. In his book *Critique of Pure Reason*, he comes up with two key objections.

It is useful to understand the way that sentences are made up of subjects and predicates. The subject is what the sentence is about; the predicate gives a description of it. 'This book is a revision guide' tells us that the subject is 'this book' and the predicate or description is that it is a revision guide.

Exam tip

Try to use Kant's own language so that you come across better to your readers.

Objection 1

Kant begins by supposing that it is true that existence is part of what it means for God to be perfect. Kant uses the example of a triangle: we know that having three angles is part of what it means for a triangle to be a triangle.

- Kant says that this example comes from a 'judgement' and not from the triangle and its existence.
- A judgement, however, is not the same as the absolute necessity of something.
- The triangle, therefore, only has three angles *if* the triangle exists in the first place.
- For Kant, ontological arguments are bad logic because they make us suppose that if we justify God's perfection as including existence we are assuming that God exists: it is circular logic.
- We can make up an object and define it in any number of ways, but this does not make the object exist in reality, even though the definition will continue to be true!

So, Kant ultimately says that if God exists, then God necessarily exists – but if God does not exist then he does not necessarily exist! Or, in other terms, you can accept the predicate of a sentence all you want, but if the subject doesn't exist in the first place, then there is no possible contradiction.

Key word

Determining predicate A description that adds something to the understanding about the subject

Objection 2

Kant's second objection is about the nature of existence as a predicate. Kant does not believe that existence is a proper predicate (a **determining predicate**).

Kant was arguing that to say 'this book is a revision guide' tells me about this book, but to say 'this book exists' does not tell me anything about the book. In this case, the book does exist, but take the idea of unicorns – 'a unicorn has a single horn' tells me what a unicorn is, but 'a unicorn exists' tells me nothing new about unicorns.

Kant's own example is of a hundred *thalers* – a currency of his day. He says that a hundred real thalers is exactly the same number of coins as a hundred possible thalers – the description is the same. The existence of the thalers is not something that can be defined by logic – it is defined by the experience of having them; thus a priori arguments cannot be said to work.

So, Kant's approach is to say that thinkers who put forward ontological arguments are treating existence in completely the wrong way.

Revision activity

Write a paragraph to explain how Kant challenges the logic of the ontological argument. Try to refer to the argument from Anselm as you go through.

Now test yourself

6 According to Kant, what can you reject in order not to need to discuss the predicate?
7 What was the currency that Kant used in his second objection?

TESTED

4.5 Assessing the ontological argument

Can existence be treated as a predicate?

Kant's view clearly was that existence is not a determining predicate and therefore does not give us information in the same way that other predicates might. Likewise, Gaunilo was suspicious of Anselm because Anselm seemed to be defining things into existence – his lost island had plenty of predicates, but not existence.

A response can be found in Anselm's *In reply to Gaunilo* where he observes that in the case of God we can say existence is a predicate because we are attributing existence in divine terms to God – perfect existence, perhaps. In the twentieth century, Norman Malcolm developed this idea and said that contingent existence (the existence of objects or beings that cannot exist) is different to necessary existence because it shows God as the special case. Contingent existence does not add information in the way that saying I have dark hair and someone else has fair hair does, but necessary existence does add information.

Kant's argument in his first objection would still stand, however. A predicate is only a predicate because it has a subject, so if the subject is rejected in the first place then there is no case to answer.

> **Exam tip**
>
> It is important to remember that you can use material on Anselm, Gaunilo and Kant if asked whether existence is a predicate.

Are there logical fallacies in this argument?

Objections to the ontological argument challenge the internal logic of the argument as a whole. There are some key areas to consider:

- Can God be defined into existence?
- Is Anselm's definition of God as the greatest possible being appropriate? Anselm does not define greatness and different people define greatness in different ways.
- Is a greatest possible being logical?
- Is it fair to say that everyone has a common understanding of God in their minds?
- Is the argument as a whole a play on words? Is the existence of someone the same as the essence of that person?
- If God can be experienced in any way then is the ontological argument needed?

> **Revision activity**
>
> Write a sentence or two to elaborate on each of these bullet points. Use scholars directly if you can.

Does the ontological argument justify belief?

These issues aside, it is clear that the ontological argument does not say anything about the nature of God and whether the God of the ontological argument is worthy of worship. However, this could be said of all the arguments for God's existence – none of them gives a full picture of God, but each could give someone a reason to learn more about God and religious belief.

The purpose of Anselm's writing was to give glory and praise to God – *Proslogion* is addressed to God. It could be argued that it is a meditation on God's existence for the believer more than a proof to the non-believer. Certainly, the ontological argument on its own is unlikely to convince the atheist of the existence of God.

The assumption here is that the believer *should* know everything about God. Many religious people are comfortable with getting glimpses of God – the challenge of faith, which is very different from reason, is to use those glimpses to live out daily life.

> **Now test yourself**
>
> 8 To whom is *Proslogion* addressed?
>
> TESTED

4.6 Comparing a priori and a posteriori arguments

The two chapters on the existence of God have explored very different arguments. A posteriori arguments start with physical evidence in the world to come to conclusions, whereas a priori arguments deduce entirely separately to experience. If it were possible to prove God's existence a priori then there would be a lack of doubt – logical proofs, just like in mathematics, are difficult to contradict. A posteriori arguments all suffer from issues of interpretation – experiences can be interpreted differently – I may say it is a nice day at the moment, but you may disagree.

A priori arguments are better	A posteriori arguments are better
Our experience can always deceive us. For example, we may be unwell or psychological factors might influence us	Aquinas rejected a priori ontological arguments because you cannot know the nature of God so cannot follow Anselm's argument through
A priori arguments work within defined terms and so the logic is easier to follow through	Hume rejected the ontological argument because you cannot think of a being that cannot not exist – you can always think of that being not existing. You would need to experience it first
Modern forms of the ontological argument are more convincing than traditional ones	People naturally work from experience first
Experiences and observations of the world are unreliable and only pure logic can be reliable	It is likely that God's handiwork would be evident in the world around us in some way

There are, of course, a number of similarities we can draw on. Both styles of argument are just that – philosophical arguments. Whatever their starting points, the internal coherence of the arguments need to be assessed. A posteriori arguments are accused of containing logical fallacies as much as ontological arguments. Equally, what might be a leap in logic for one person might not be for another.

The alternative approach is to see all the arguments as doing a different aspect of the same job – like looking at something from a variety of angles. If the starting point is that it is impossible fully to know God, who is beyond description, then the arguments can be seen as limited ways of understanding God. However, the philosopher Antony Flew pointed out that 'if one leaky bucket will not hold water there is no reason to suppose that ten can'. Any number of flawed arguments cannot prove God.

Some would reject arguments as a whole because any use of logic to try to understand God is invalid. Human logic cannot ever fully understand God and we must rely on God's decision to reveal himself to us if we want to know about him. However, it could then be said that God's revelation of himself to us is actually the starting point for a posteriori arguments.

Clearly, to a religious believer, the arguments are likely to affirm faith. The a posteriori arguments could draw on experiences that a believer has had; the a priori approach could act like Anselm first intended it – as a meditation on faith. To an atheist or agnostic, however, it is unlikely that any words on paper will work.

> **Revision activity**
>
> Try to rank order the arguments for each of a priori and a posteriori thought. Does one come out as more convincing than the other?

> **Making links**
>
> Look at the difference between natural and revealed theology in the Developments in Christian Thought book, Chapter 3.

Now test yourself

9 Who suggested that ten leaky buckets do not hold water, so ten arguments for God's existence that are flawed do not prove his existence?

Exam checklist

- Explain Anselm's ontological argument.
- Explain how Gaunilo challenged Anselm's argument.
- Evaluate Kant's approach to the argument.
- Compare a priori and a posteriori arguments.
- Analyse the idea that existence is a predicate.
- Evaluate whether the ontological argument justifies belief.

Sample work

Not all exam questions will state a scholar's name or the title of an argument. It is important in your preparation that you take note of all the different phrases used in the specification – we have tried to mirror them as much as we can in the headings and sub-headings of the book. Imagine an essay question that talks about existence being a predicate. In the pressure of the moment in the examination, you would have to remember that this is an essay on the ontological argument; and once you've done that, you would need to keep bringing each paragraph you write back to the wording in the question.

First attempt	Improvement
Kant says that if we imagine a £5 note and we have a £5 note, the amount of money is the same, but having it in reality does not add anything to our understanding of £5. Thus, Kant criticises the ontological argument.	Kant uses the example of 100 thalers. He says that 100 real thalers have no more thalers in them than 100 possible ones and so the existence of the thalers does not change the description of the thalers – and so existence is not a real predicate. Thus, in rejecting the ontological argument's use of existence, Kant rejects the idea that existence is a predicate.

Going further: Descartes' argument

Rene Descartes (1596–1650) gives a version of the ontological argument that can help with our understanding of Kant's objections. Famous for saying, 'I think, therefore I am', Descartes shied away from using evidence from the senses, because rational thought was so much more reliable than sensory thought.

- A triangle is determined by having three angles which add up to two right angles (180 degrees).
- This has been the case even before we knew the fact.
- In the same way, God, who is a 'supremely perfect being', must exist – his existence is as fundamental to his essence (being God) as having angles adding up to two right angles is to being a triangle.
- Another analogy is a mountain requiring a valley – the two go together, just like God and existence.
- But thinking of the mountain and the valley does not make them exist, just like thinking of a winged horse does not make it exist.
- However, God is different, because the mountain and valley still go together if they don't exist; God and existence still go together (the word 'God' essentially means 'the existing God exists') – and so God exists.

Exam tip

Descartes' argument (or any other versions that you have studied in class) can be used freely in the exam as long as they are relevant to the question!

5 Religious experience

5.1 Introduction

Religious experience is different to many of the topics in the Philosophy of Religion unit. While a number of topics are abstract and theoretical, this topic begins with claims that the divine can be encountered and known directly. Religious experience is a widespread phenomenon. In his book *Religious Experience Today*, David Hay suggested that around 30 per cent of the population has had something resembling a religious experience. In this topic, we will examine different types of religious experience, such as mystical experiences and conversion experiences. There are different understandings of what we should conclude about such experiences: are they genuine encounters with a greater power or might they have psychological or physiological explanations? One of the difficulties in assessing religious experiences is that they are private experiences of one individual in most cases; the topic therefore also looks at whether shared corporate experiences effectively answer this objection.

The specification says

Topic	Content	Key knowledge
Religious experience	The nature and influence of religious experience, including: ● mystical experience ● conversion experience	Examples of mystical and conversion experiences and views about these, including: ● views and main conclusions of William James
	Different ways in which individual religious experiences can be understood	● as union with a greater power ● psychological effect such as illusion ● the product of a physiological effect
	Learners should have the opportunity to discuss issues related to arguments for the existence of God based on reason, including: ● whether personal testimony or witness is enough to support the validity of religious experiences ● whether or not corporate religious experiences might be considered more reliable or valid than individual experiences ● whether or not religious experience provides a basis for belief in God or a greater power.	

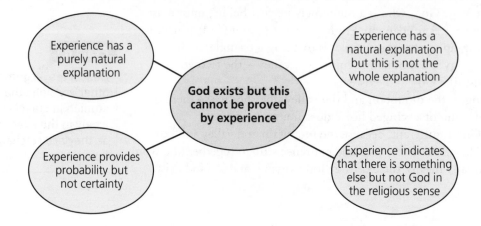

5.2 William James

One of the leading thinkers in the area of religious experience is the philosopher and psychologist William James (1842–1910). His book *The Varieties of Religious Experience* aims to provide a survey of different types of religious experiences and to suggest what we may infer from them. In studying religious experience, James argues that we are studying the very heart of religion, whereas studying beliefs and practices is merely second-hand religion. Beliefs and practices develop later as people reflect on their experiences within their theological system.

Religion and the mind

James accepts that there may be a psychological or physiological explanation to religious experience. Yet he argues that this may not be the whole explanation. Even if there is a natural cause of the experience, there may also be a supernatural one behind it. What is important when we judge whether experiences are genuine is not what causes them (their root), but the effects that they have (their fruit). In one example he gives, just because it is possible that Paul's conversion (see page 42) was an epileptic episode, this does not mean that it was not also a genuine religious experience; his changed life after the experience counts as evidence for this.

> **Key quote**
>
> Be ready now to judge the religious life by its results exclusively.
>
> James, *The Varieties of Religious Experience*

The characteristics of religious experience

James suggests that the following four features are common to all religious experiences, particularly mystical experiences

1 They are **ineffable**. The experience is beyond proper description. Words cannot express what is felt. James suggests that this is the most obvious mark of religious experiences. He states that such as only a musician can truly hear a symphony and only someone who has been in love understands love, so too this ineffable encounter has to be directly experienced.
2 Religious experiences have a **noetic** quality: the person who has the experience feels that they have gained a deep and direct knowledge of God. It is a knowledge deeper than that of everyday events. These revelations provide what James calls a 'curious sense of authority'.
3 The experience is **transient**. It passes with time, usually lasting for half an hour or less but the effects of the experience may be long lasting.
4 There is a sense of **passivity** in the experience: the experiencer has a sense that something is acting upon them; they are not contributing anything to the experience. They may take a step such as focusing their attention or engaging in breathing exercises, but the experience itself cannot be summoned. The believer has the sense that they are 'grasped and held by a superior power'.

> **Key words**
>
> **Ineffable** Unable to be expressed or described in words, beyond description
>
> **Noetic** Having the property of imparting knowledge
>
> **Transient** An event that passes with time, temporary
>
> **Passivity** The idea that the person having the religious experience is not taking the leading role; they are being 'acted upon'

James' key principles on religious experience

James' conclusions about religious experience rest on several key principles

1 **Pragmatism**. James is a pragmatist in terms of his understanding of the idea of truth. Truth is not something that is fixed but rather 'true' is whatever has value for us and works in real life. Hence given the effects of religious experiences, we ought to conclude that they are probably true.

> **Key word**
>
> **Pragmatism** A philosophical movement that argues that a theory must be treated as true if it works in practice

2 **Empiricism**. James is committed to an empirical approach. Although we cannot empirically verify the experience, the result of the experience is empirical data. If a former criminal is now living a good and religious life following a conversion experience, this can be observed by our senses.

3 **Pluralism**. James' research into experiences in different faiths led him to conclude that there were similarities. These experiences may be interpreted differently dependent on our own views and belief systems but if they produce positive effects then they are in some sense true. Hence there is truth in all faiths.

Key words

Empiricism The idea that observations via our senses lead us to understanding of the world

Pluralism The idea in religion that truth is to be found in many faiths

Key quotes

I think it may be asserted that there are religious experiences of a specific nature ... I think that they point with reasonable probability to the continuity of our consciousness with a wider, spiritual environment from which the ordinary man is shut off.

I feel bound to say that religious experience, as we have studied it, cannot be cited as unequivocally supporting the infinitist belief.

The only thing that it unequivocally testifies to is that we can experience union with something larger than ourselves and in that union find our greatest peace.

James, *The Varieties of Religious Experience*

What might religious experience show?

As the quotes show, William James stops short of suggesting that religious experiences prove God. Waking consciousness is only one type of consciousness and there are other forms of consciousness that those having religious experiences can access. James draws an analogy with drunkenness; a drunk is put into another state by alcohol. So too a mystic may be able to access different states of consciousness. Not everyone is able to access these experiences; James distinguishes between the ordinary man and the spiritual man. At the end of *The Varieties of Religious Experience*, James himself offers these conclusions:

1 The world we see is part of a more spiritual universe from which it gets its main significance.
2 To unite with this higher universe is our true end or purpose.
3 Prayer or meditation is a real process where spiritual energy flows and produces psychological and material effects within the world we see.
4 Religion seems to provide people with a new zest for life and/or provides purpose.
5 An assurance of safety and a sense of peace and love in relationships to others is also produced.

Now test yourself   TESTED

1 According to William James, what is the key test for the genuineness of a religious experience?
2 What are James' four characteristics of a religious experience?

5.3 Mystical experiences

For many thinkers, including William James, religious experience is primarily mystical in nature. This is a difficult term to describe but essentially **mystical experience** tends to seek the unity of all things. There are groups that value mystical experiences in all of the major world faiths.

Happold's conclusions on mysticism

A relatively recent study of mystical experiences was undertaken by F.C. Happold (1893–1971), which draws several key conclusions.
- Mystics understand this world as only part of ultimate reality; the world comes from a 'Divine Ground'.
- This 'Divine Ground' can be known intuitively but not rationally.
- We are comprised of our 'ego' and our 'eternal self'. It is this latter aspect of us that has the divine spark, the ability to connect with deeper truths.
- Our purpose is to discover our true 'eternal self' and unite with the 'Divine Ground'.

> **Key word**
>
> **Mystical experience** A direct experience of God or ultimate reality, a sense of oneness of all things

> **Key quote**
>
> One may say truly, I think, that personal religious experience has its root and centre in mystical states of consciousness.
>
> James, *The Varieties of Religious Experience*

St Teresa of Avila

One prominent example of mystical experiences within Christianity comes from the writings of St Teresa of Avila (1515–1582). In her writings, she argues that experiences should be subject to tests to determine whether they are genuine. These tests include whether there is a positive change in the person, whether the experience left the person at peace rather than disturbed, and whether the experience fits with the teachings of the church.

Example

> I was at prayer on a festival of the glorious Saint Peter when I saw Christ at my side, or, to put it better, I was conscious of Him, for neither with the eyes of the body or of the soul did I see anything. I thought He was quite close to me and I saw that it was He who, as I thought, was speaking to me … All the time Jesus Christ seemed to be beside me … I could not discern in what form.
>
> St Teresa of Avila

Otto on numinous experiences

One thinker who challenges the idea that religious experience is intimate or shows the unity of all things is Rudolf Otto (1869–1937). In his book, *The Idea of the Holy*, he describes what he calls a **numinous experience**. These experiences are experiences of awe and wonder in the presence of an almighty God. In it, we are not so much united with God but aware of our own insignificance in his presence.

Otto uses the phrase *Mysterium: tremendum et fascinans* to describe these experiences. They are:
- mysterious
- tremendous and terrifying
- fascinating and compelling.

He argues that all religious experience is numinous in nature. However, it is a matter of debate among philosophers whether numinous experiences are a completely different type of experience or are just a type of mystical experience.

> **Key word**
>
> **Numinous experience** An experience of awe and wonder in the presence of an almighty God

5.4 Conversion experiences

William James on conversion

- **Centre of energy**. A **conversion** involves someone altering their beliefs and way of life. It is similar to what may happen gradually over time in what James refers to as the shifting of energies. An example of this may be that our entire thoughts are taken over by rock music, but this is gradually replaced by a passion for politics. James' own example involves the President who, while fishing on a day off, gives little thought to political matters. In a religious conversion, religious beliefs and identity come to be at the centre of a person's consciousness.
- **Psychology**. James' views on conversion fit with his general ideas on religious experience. There is undoubtedly a psychological explanation of conversion – James suggests that the subconscious may be active in a similar way to when someone is in a hypnotic state – but this psychological explanation need not be the whole explanation.

> **Key word**
>
> **Conversion** An experience which causes a sudden or gradual change in someone's belief system

> **Key quote**
>
> To say that a man is 'converted' means in these terms that religious ideas, previously peripheral in his consciousness, now take a central place, and that religious aims form the habitual centre of his energy.
> James, *The Varieties of Religious Experience*

> **Key quote**
>
> In the Bible, the apostle Paul recounts his conversion experience which changed him from a persecutor of the early Christians to one of its greatest leaders:
>
> About noon as I came near Damascus, suddenly a bright light from heaven flashed around me. I fell to the ground and heard a voice say to me, 'Saul! Saul! Why do you persecute me?'
>
> 'Who are you, Lord?' I asked.
>
> 'I am Jesus of Nazareth, whom you are persecuting,' he replied. My companions saw the light, but they did not understand the voice of him who was speaking to me.
>
> 'What shall I do, Lord?' I asked.
>
> *Acts 22:6–10*

Edwin Starbuck on conversion

- **A parallel with adolescence**. The nineteenth-century psychologist Edwin Starbuck's study of conversion prompted him to draw parallels with the normal process of development and finding our identity in adolescence. Starbuck studied evangelical Christian conversions alongside non-religious adolescents. He found that most conversions occurred between the ages of 14 and 17 years (modern thinkers have suggested 15–24 years). All adolescents go through similar stages of a sense of incompleteness and anxiety before finding 'happy relief' and a sense of identity. Starbuck argues that religious conversion is in fact a 'normal' process of growing up and finding one's identity.
- **Two types of conversion**. These conversions can be gradual (Starbuck calls this a volitional conversion) as the religious ideas gradually take centre stage, or can be sudden (Starbuck calls this self-surrender) where possibly in response to a crisis the religious ideas dramatically replace other dominant ideas.

> **Revision activity**
>
> Using the arguments on conversion in this section, practise turning the bullet points into paragraphs. Aim to assess each point rather than merely stating it.

Arguments on conversion

- William James: Judge the experience by the fruit (its effects).
- Edwin Starbuck: Similar to normal adolescence.
- Sigmund Freud: Conversions as hallucinations, wishful thinking.
- Antony Flew: Conversions are almost always to a religion the person has grown up with.
- Richard Swinburne: Principles of credulity and testimony.

> **Now test yourself**
>
> 3 What is a conversion experience?
> 4 What did Starbuck discover about conversion experiences?
>
> TESTED

5.5 The case for religious experience

Religious experience as union with a higher power

Some thinkers have argued that religious experiences are genuine experiences of a higher power. There are several possible arguments that can be given.

- **The effects**. The effects of religious experiences can be significant and often highly positive (although not always). William James argues that this 'judging of the fruit' is the only possible test for religious experiences. It is argued that a natural explanation is inadequate to explain these effects.
- **The volume**. If religious experiences were more rare, they could be dismissed more easily. Yet there is a significant volume of religious experiences. It is claimed by David Hay in his book, *Religious Experience Today*, that around 30 per cent of people questioned have had experience of 'a powerful spiritual force'.
- **Similarities**. There are considerable similarities of description that would not be present if people were making up or imagining their accounts.

Swinburne's case for religious experience

Richard Swinburne (1934–) presents two arguments to suggest that we ought to give religious experience the benefit of the doubt.

1 **The principle of credulity**. We should accept what appears to be the case unless we have clear evidence to the contrary.

2 **The principle of testimony**. We should believe that what others tell us happened probably did happen unless we have a good reason not to – for instance, they are untrustworthy or under the influence of something.

Responding to the argument

The points given above are not convincing to the sceptic response.

- Religious experiences are different to ordinary experiences. They are not empirical but are usually private to the individual's mind. Hence it is unwise to give them the benefit of the doubt.
- Peter Donovan draws a distinction between 'feeling certain' and 'being right'. When a believer claims to know God through religious experience, they are merely saying that they feel certain. The claim is subjective.
- Experiences are interpreted quite differently by followers of different faiths and this leads to different and conflicting truth claims.

Is testimony enough to support the validity of religious experience?

One related question to the issue of whether religious experience is a genuine encounter with a higher power involves the principle of testimony outlined above. Can we really give religious experiences the benefit of the doubt as Swinburne would want us to do?

- In everyday life, we evaluate people's claims by a number of factors: we may consider the reputation or past reliability of an individual, whether they were in a good state to perceive what they claim (for example, were they drunk or mentally ill)? We may also consider whether the individual in question has a bias or has something to gain from the claim they are making.

> **Typical mistake**
>
> Candidates will commonly write that thinkers such as James and Swinburne prove or attempt to prove the existence of God. Yet both thinkers are careful to suggest that the evidence is not that clear cut and that religious experience at best makes God probable but not certain.

- American philosopher Caroline Franks-Davis argues that while we can take everyday claims at face value, the issue of religious experience is not a trivial one and thus deserves a more critical treatment.
- William James and others would argue that the testimony alone is not sufficient to prove an experience genuine. The after-effects in terms of character and lifestyle – the 'fruit' – are more important. However, Bertrand Russell argued that even a good effect is not necessarily evidence; good effects on character can be produced by fictional characters in books.

5.6 Do religious experiences have a psychological or physiological explanation?

REVISED

The psychological explanation of religious experiences

Some thinkers have argued that religious experiences are not genuine and that psychological explanations, such as illusion, can be given.

- The nineteenth-century atheist philosopher Ludwig Feuerbach (1804–1872) argued that the idea of God is a human invention. All the attributes of God – such as power, knowledge and goodness – can be seen in human nature. We project and stretch these human qualities to create the idea of God. We create God in our image – 'God is man written in large letters.' This idea of God is passed down through generations.
- This idea had a great impact on Sigmund Freud (1856–1939), who argued that religious behaviour was a neurosis caused by childhood insecurities. The idea of a God existing is psychologically attractive as our wrongdoing can be forgiven and we have hope in the face of death. Religious experiences are therefore hallucinations that are caused by deep subconscious desires in the same way as dreams when we are asleep.

A response to the psychological challenge

William James argued that even if religious experiences have a psychological explanation, this does not mean that a supernatural explanation is ruled out. Carl Gustav Jung (1875–1961) accepted religious experience and responded to Freud by suggesting that the development of our spiritual aspect was essential to psychological wholeness. He claimed that each of us has the archetype (idea) of God from within a shared collective unconscious.

The physiological explanation of religious experiences

In recent years, there has been considerable interest in physiological explanations of religious experience as a result of work in biology, specifically neuroscience.

- Richard Dawkins (1941–) has suggested that religious ideas may be 'memes'. Similar to the way that genes work, these are ideas that as we have evolved have been useful to our survival, hence our brain accepts them more readily. They are reproduced within our brains. Dawkins refers to religion as a 'virus of the mind'. Religious experience can be explained entirely by reference to the physical brain.
- The work of Newberg and D'Aquili has suggested that there are neuropsychological mechanisms which lie beneath religious experiences. They carried out a number of experiments using brain scans on meditating Buddhist monks. They refer to the 'causal operator' and the 'holistic operator' which operate within the brain. These seem to show an increased level of activity during meditation.

> **Key quote**
>
> If you eat too little, you see visions; if you drink too much, you see snakes.
>
> Bertrand Russell

- Michael Persinger's (1945–) experiment involving the 'God helmet' has also aroused interest. In this experiment, volunteers wore a helmet that generated a magnetic field around their brain. A significant proportion of the participants reported feelings that were similar to those in religious experiences.

A response

As with the psychological challenge the fact that there is a physical dimension to religious experience need not lead us to reject the experience completely. On a physical level, our ordinary experiences, such as hearing birds sing, can be reduced to neurological events but that does not mean the birds are not real. In the same way, it may be that God is causing our experiences, and using our 'holistic operator' to do it.

5.7 Corporate experiences: are they more reliable than individual experiences?

REVISED

Corporate religious experiences are experiences that are shared by a number of people. Given that one of the issues involved in studying religious experiences is that experiences are private to individuals, **corporate experiences** are interesting as potentially there may be some external verification of the experience.

Examples of corporate religious experiences

There are a number of famous examples of corporate religious experience.
- **Fatima**. In Fatima, Portugal, in 1917 a crowd of over 30,000 gathered in response to visions that claimed that a miracle would occur on that day. As the crowd looked up to the sky reports claim that they witnessed the sun 'dancing' and making strange movements in the sky.
- **Medjugorje**. In June 1981, six children experienced visions of the Virgin Mary over a period of several days. The children each claim to have received secrets and have had repeated visions in the years since.
- **Toronto Blessing**. In the 1990s, a phenomenon known as the Toronto Blessing began at Toronto Airport Christian Fellowship and subsequently spread worldwide. The most widely reported part of this was uncontrollable 'holy laughter' as well as crying, shrieking, and falling to the floor – 'slain in the spirit'. Christians claimed that they were acting under the influence of the Holy Spirit.

Objections to corporate religious experiences

In addition to the standard arguments for and against religious experiences (pages 43–44), there are several other objections that are specifically relevant to corporate experiences.
- **Mass hysteria**. One psychological objection to corporate religious experience comes from the phenomenon of mass hysteria or collective hysteria. In these cases, a group of people can spontaneously start to generate physical symptoms in response to a psychological stimulus such as fear. Throughout history, there have been a number of cases where a large number of people have become convinced they have caught some serious illness and have displayed symptoms that upon analysis were shown to be purely psychological. It is suggested that the style of worship in some evangelical Christian churches might trigger this type of phenomenon.
- **Trivial acts**. One of the concerns about reports of the Toronto Blessing and the events at Fatima is that some of the claimed acts of God seem incredibly trivial or random. It seems strange that if God were to

Now test yourself

5 What is the principle of testimony and why do some thinkers criticise this principle?
6 How do psychologists such as Freud criticise religious experience?
7 What is the God helmet and how might it challenge religious experience?

TESTED

Key word

Corporate experience An experience that is shared by a group

intervene in the world or directly communicate with humans that these events would take place rather than more useful miracles or messages.

● Although it may seem that experiences are shared, it can be objected that in reality there is not a shared experience but there are lots of individual experiences; no one can fully know what is happening inside another person's mind.

5.8 Religious experience as a basis for believing in God or a greater power

REVISED

In order to argue that religious experience provides proof or, at the very least, strong evidence for the existence of God, the following two assumptions need to be made.

1 Experiences are genuine and cannot be explained in a natural way.
2 It is God that is causing these experiences.

Are these genuine experiences that cannot be explained naturally?

Feuerbach and Freud have argued that a psychological explanation of experience is possible based on projection and wishful thinking. Dawkins and Persinger have drawn attention to the physiological factors in religious experience that have been discovered in modern neuroscience. However, it is worth noting that for William James this is not necessarily a fatal objection; it may be that the natural explanation is not the full explanation.

Is it God that is causing these experiences?

Even if experiences are genuine and have no other obvious explanation, it is still quite a step to claim that the explanation must be God.

● **Interpretation and conflicting truth claims**. It may be that all experiencers encounter the same thing but interpret it differently. This is fine in general terms for Judaism, Christianity and Islam where the idea of God is broadly similar, but not all religions have a monotheistic God. There is a belief in many gods in popular Hinduism and most forms of Buddhism are atheistic. Is God at work in all faiths? Do some misinterpret him because of their existing beliefs? Are some experiences false?

● **Particularity**. If this is God who is causing the experiences, it raises an interesting theological objection as God is choosing some for experiences and not others. Would it not be better if God revealed himself to all or none rather than show favouritism?

● **Logical problems**. If there is a God, he is logically 'wholly other' to human beings. This leads some thinkers such as Kant to suggest that religious experience is logically impossible. However, while it may be impossible for us to reach God, there is no reason why God cannot choose to reveal himself to us in a way that we can comprehend.

Note that both steps in the argument are fraught with difficulties as in addition to the issues above, religious experiences are logically private and are ineffable in nature. Hence it is not an easy phenomenon to draw conclusions about.

5.9 Summary and exam tips

Exam checklist

- Explain using examples what is meant by mystical experiences, numinous experiences and conversion experiences.
- Explain the views of William James and his main conclusions about religious experience.
- Explain and assess different understandings of religious experience, including the views that they are genuine, they are psychological or they are physiological.
- Assess whether testimonies of religious experience are enough to confirm their validity.
- Assess whether corporate religious experiences are more reliable than individual experiences.
- Consider whether religious experiences enable us to believe in the existence of God or a higher power.

Sample work

REVISED

The topic of religious experience allows the use of examples to illustrate points. One of the dangers is that an overly long description of a religious experience can take time and detract from the point you are making. Remember that the point of each of your paragraphs has to be providing an explanation (AO1) and/or evaluating arguments (AO2). The example should support this.

Basic long paragraph	Better short paragraph
A corporate religious experience is an experience that is shared by many people. One example of a corporate religious experience is the Toronto Blessing. This happened at the Toronto Airport Vineyard Church in 1994. During a sermon given by pastor Rodney Howard Browne, the congregation experienced uncontrollable laughter, speaking in tongues and were slain in the spirit (they fell to the floor) when prayed for. This phenomenon known as the Toronto Blessing spread throughout a number of evangelical churches across the world. Supporters of the movement said that this demonstrated that God was at work. Comment: This is quite descriptive. Description is a lower level skill than showing understanding of something.	The issue of the private nature of religious experience is avoided in corporate religious experiences where an experience is shared between several or many individuals. A famous example of this is the 1994 Toronto Blessing where congregations seemed to spontaneously speak in tongues, laugh uncontrollably and were slain in the spirit following prayer. The shared nature of the experience arguably provides greater evidence for God's work than a solitary experience. Comment: Here an example is given but the focus is on using the example to further the point.

Going further: Personal knowledge

When philosophers argue that religious experience brings 'knowledge of God' they tend to widen the idea of what knowledge is; it is not just about things that we experience.

Personal knowledge. Philosophical arguing that religious experience provides personal knowledge may draw the distinction between knowing about someone and experiencing them directly. We would have a deeper knowledge of the prime minister if we met her for an hour than if we just read about her in books. In the same way, religious experience provides deeper knowledge of God. The Jewish philosopher Martin Buber expands upon this by describing religious experience as an I–thou relationship, a direct person-to-person encounter as opposed to an I–it relationship where another person may effectively be an object to us.

OCR A Level Religious Studies: Philosophy of Religion   47

6 The problem of evil

6.1 Introduction

REVISED

Evil and suffering seem to be the greatest challenge to religious belief. How can God let it happen? For some, it is enough to reject the existence of a theistic God entirely; for others, it is something that can be explained through **theodicy**. In this chapter, we look at two approaches to theodicy.

Evil is usually divided into:
- **moral evil** – evil that is a result of the free actions of humans (e.g. murder)
- **natural evil** – evil that comes from nature that humans cannot stop (e.g. earthquakes).

The two types of evil should not be seen as clearly distinguished: sometimes they might overlap, such as when a natural evil comes from human activity.

The consequence of evil is **suffering** and evil is a problem because of the amount of suffering it causes – how many people suffer, how bad the suffering is and so on. **Innocent suffering** in particular challenges the believer to ask how God can allow innocent people to suffer.

The religious believer seems to be challenged more by natural evil than moral evil, because moral evil can be explained by the sinful actions of others. In philosophy of religion, the process of theodicy tries to explain why God can still be believed in and worshipped despite evil being in the world. Augustine explained evil as a result of free choices of people and Hick found the meaning of evil in the way that people freely choose to respond to suffering – both place free will at the centre of their theories.

The specification says

> **Key words**
>
> **Theodicy** A theory to justify God's righteousness (when faced with evil)
>
> **Moral evil** Evil that is a result of human free choices
>
> **Natural evil** Evil that comes from nature or natural sources
>
> **Suffering** Pain or harm experienced by a person
>
> **Innocent suffering** The suffering experienced by those who do not deserve it

> **Key quote**
>
> And if the suffering of children goes to make up the sum of suffering needed to buy truth, then I assert beforehand that the whole of truth is not worth such a price.
>
> Dostoyevsky, *The Brothers Karamazov*

Topic	Content	Key knowledge
The problem of evil	The problem of evil and suffering: • different presentations	• including its logical (the inconsistency between divine attributes and the presence of evil) and evidential (the evidence of so much terrible evil in the world) aspects
	• theodicies that propose some justification or reason for divine action or inaction in the face of evil	• Augustine's use of original perfection and the Fall • Hick's reworking of the Irenaean theodicy, which gives some purpose to natural evil in enabling human beings to reach divine likeness
	Learners should have the opportunity to discuss issues related to the problem of evil, including: • whether or not Augustine's view of the origins of moral and natural evils is enough to spare God from blame for evils in the world • whether or not the need to create a 'vale of soul-making' can justify the existence or extent of evils • which of the logical or evidential aspects of the problem of evil pose the greater challenge to belief • whether or not it is possible to successfully defend monotheism in the face of evil.	

Now test yourself

TESTED

1 Sort these examples of evil into moral and natural evils: tornadoes, theft, genocide, tsunamis, poverty, pollution.
2 What is meant by the word 'theodicy'?

6.2 The logical and evidential problems of evil

The logical problem of evil

Evil is a problem for the believer, not because it challenges the existence of God but because it challenges the nature of God and so is logically a problem. Theistic religions believe God to be all-powerful and all-loving and yet evil exists:

- How can God be all-powerful (omnipotent) and not stop evil?
- How can God be all-loving ([omni]benevolent) and not want to stop evil?

This problem was stated first like this by Epicurus in the third century BCE and is a standard approach to this question. In order for this **inconsistent triad** to be resolved, it seems that one of the three parts of it (omnipotence, benevolence and evil) must not be true, as these possible solutions show:

- Perhaps God is not omnipotent and cannot control evil (or human free choices) – this is the view of process theology.
- Perhaps God is not benevolent and God's benevolence is a view that has just come from the New Testament focus on love. The Old Testament God's view of justice seems to be fair, but brutal – for example, in the way God fights for the people of Israel.
- Perhaps our definitions of omnipotence and benevolence need to change.
- Perhaps evil does not exist as we think it does – it is not a substance like goodness is.

The evidential problem of evil

Evil is evidentially a problem because it can be seen in the evidence of people's suffering, especially in the quantity of suffering and in the fact that innocent people suffer. It might make a religious believer question why God, who knows everything, would allow it to happen.

- Natural disasters can displace, injure or kill many thousands of people at a time.
- Moral evil can cause some humans to perform acts that for others are unthinkable.
- Suffering takes place in nature in ways that we don't always think about: animals kill and eat other animals to survive, for example.

If God really knows everything, why did he create the universe knowing that extreme examples of evil and suffering would occur? What could possibly make up for the suffering in the world?

Some responses

- Perhaps evil is part of a 'big picture plan' that God has for the world and should not be taken at face value.
- Some suffering is good because it teaches us to learn from our mistakes or it warns us that something worse might happen.
- Suffering and evil can bring out the best in people.
- Perhaps God needs to test humans in some way.
- Suffering could be a result of the previous actions of people, i.e. a form of punishment.
- If we are to be allowed to be genuinely free, then suffering is something we have to accept in some way.
- The Bible suggests that there comes a point where we have to 'let go' of our intellectual questioning about evil and suffering and accept the love of God.

> **Key word**
>
> **Inconsistent triad** A triad (three things) of items that do not seem to be able all to be true at the same time – in this case, God being all-powerful, all-loving and evil existing

> **Exam tip**
>
> It is useful to have general responses such as these to help detailed analysis of points, although you will need to know Augustine and Hick in enough detail to write essays just on these thinkers.

> **Now test yourself**
>
> 3 Why is evil logically a problem for the religious believer?
>
> TESTED

6.3 Augustine

Augustine (354–430) was a bishop who saw evil and suffering as coming out of free will.

Original perfection

Augustine believed that a perfect God could only create a perfect world, as seen in the creation stories in the Bible. Each thing is good in its own way – a flower is good for a flower, for example. This led him to say that evil is an absence or **privation** of good (the Latin phrase is *privatio boni*). In the same way that blindness is an absence of sight or darkness is a lack of light, so evil is a falling short of good.

The Fall

Augustine saw the story of the **Fall** as central to understanding why humans have an absence of good in themselves. Even before Adam and Eve, some angels, having been made perfect, misused their free will and fell from God's grace and so hell was created and the harmony of creation disturbed. In the Garden of Eden, Adam and Eve disobeyed God's command by giving in to temptation and they too broke the harmonious relationship with God. All evil in the world stems from these acts of disobedience.

Augustine's theodicy

According to Augustine:
- Everything is created perfectly by God.
- However, all things fall short of this perfection due to the Fall of both angels and humans.
- This led to a loss of harmony in nature, which in turns leads to natural evil.
- People continue to fall short and this leads to moral evil.
- All humans deserve to be punished for the Original Sin of Adam and Eve and for their continuing sinfulness.
- We deserve this because we are all 'seminally present in the loins of Adam' – we are all descendants of Adam and Eve and so share in the effects of Original Sin.
- As God is fair and just he cannot stop evil and suffering because he cannot interfere with free actions.
- However, he sent Jesus to earth as a sign of his grace to give the opportunity for people to go to heaven.
- Just like a picture is improved by good use of shadows, so too is evil part of the natural balance of the universe and from God's perspective the universe is aesthetically pleasing because it is beautiful and balanced. A world with evil and genuine free will is better than a world without choice: Augustine compared this to a runaway horse, which is better than a stone that stays in place by itself because the stone has no movement or perception of its own.

For Augustine, evil comes ultimately from the Fall, affecting harmony in the world and resulting in human punishment. However, God's benevolence shows that humans have not been abandoned. For Augustine, all evil is either sin or punishment for sin. In modern terms, Augustine's theodicy is described as **soul-deciding**. We have to decide whether or not to obey God.

Making links

Augustine's approach to human nature is examined in the Developments in Christian Thought book, Chapter 1.

Key words

Privation A lack or absence of something

Fall The moment when Adam and Eve disobeyed God by eating the fruit of the forbidden tree; humans are 'fallen' because of this moment

Key word

Soul-deciding theodicy A theodicy that emphasises that evil requires a decision from humans about whether they will follow God or give in to evil

Strengths and weaknesses

Augustine's approach seems to fit with our experience of the world: free will seems to cause most suffering, so it is possible to extend this to the idea that it is the cause of all suffering, including that caused by natural evil. It certainly seems reasonable to put the emphasis on human action, not God's action. If we did not have free will and were robots, would life be at all worthwhile?

Aquinas explored natural evil further and said that it might only be evil because of the way we look at the world (a cat eating a mouse is not evil from the cat's perspective, but entirely natural). For Aquinas, the idea of death as an aspect of our punishment (death came about through the Fall) gives a motivation to humans.

The idea of privation also makes sense and emphasises the ultimate goodness of God. Privation can be supported by the idea of twentieth-century thinker Herbert McCabe, who said that a bad deckchair is not the same as a bad grape: the deckchair may be bad if it collapses when you sit on it, but that wouldn't make a grape bad! So, privation is the idea that something is bad if it falls short of our expectations for it. Some might argue that Augustine's theodicy is therefore internally coherent: evil does not mean God has fallen short of expectations; we have.

There do, however, seem to be some weaknesses to the theodicy:

- It requires a reading of *Genesis* that is not always accepted by Christians today and that is challenged by the Theory of Evolution. Evolution also suggests that over time species are adapting towards perfection; Augustine works the other way around, suggesting that we are moving away from perfection.
- If the Adam and Eve story is true and the world was created perfectly, how can they have known that they were disobeying God and choosing evil? Did they have genuine freedom to choose evil?
- The idea of humans being seminally present in Adam's loins does not seem fair or just: why should we be punished for Adam and Eve's actions?
- This point also does not tie in to our biological understanding of reproduction.
- It does not seem to make sense to say that all things were made perfectly by God and then went wrong: if they were made perfectly, why did they go wrong? Equally, if God made hell, then why did he make a place that assumed things would go wrong? This must leave part of the blame for evil with God, not placing it entirely onto humans.
- Perhaps humans are simply flawed and cannot be perfect.
- Augustine's view is that, because of the Fall, humans have a natural inclination to sin. It does not seem fair, therefore, that we can be held fully responsible for our actions, because we are no longer able to make fully free choices.
- Augustine also believed that God is in control of who goes to heaven and who goes to hell. In this case, again, human free will seems to be limited.
- It is difficult to see how angelic disobedience could have caused plate tectonics. Earthquakes happen because of the way the world was made.
- The theodicy does not help people who are suffering to understand what they are going through, nor does it explain the sheer quantities of suffering.
- Augustine's response to the suffering of innocent babies is that they are tainted by Original Sin, which some find difficult.

6.4 Hick

Irenaean theodicies

Whereas Augustine placed the emphasis on evil as a punishment, theodicies that come from the tradition of Irenaeus (who died in about the year 200) see evil as an opportunity. These theodicies are not soul-deciding but **soul-making**. They focus on the idea that evil is in the world to help people to develop their characters in some way and so evil and free will are both part of God shaping the world to perfection.

Central to this type of theodicy is the verse in *Genesis* where God creates humans both in his image and in his likeness. For Irenaeus and those who use his approach, God's likeness is something that we (as both individuals and the human race) need to achieve, or grow into, through the development of our characters because true likeness is chosen, not given, and so evil is part of a process, not just in our lifetimes, but over the whole course of human history.

> **Key word**
>
> **Soul-making theodicy** A theodicy that explains evil as a way of developing or making the soul

> **Key quote**
>
> Then God said, 'Let us make [human] kind in our image, in our likeness.'
>
> *Genesis 1:26*

Hick's reworking

John Hick (1922–2012) took free will as his starting point when considering the problem of evil. Free will must be complete and genuine and must have been given so that we can have a complete and genuine relationship with God. With true freedom comes the possibility of consequences, even if they are negative. Genuine freedom requires all possible choices and all possible consequences and needs to be free from God's intervention.

The reason behind this is Hick's idea of the **epistemic distance** between God and humanity. This gap in knowledge between us and God gives us the space we need to use our freedom fully.

For Hick, something is only good when its purpose is considered. If there were a world with no possibility of pain, that might be good on one level, but it would not be good in the sense of soul-making. This is known as an **instrumental good** – something that is good for a purpose (as opposed to an intrinsic good). This world is instrumentally good because it is good for our development into God's likeness. Hick's phrase is that the world is a 'vale of soul-making' – a place whose purpose is to make souls.

> **Key words**
>
> **Epistemic distance** The gap in knowledge between God and humanity; human inability to know God fully
>
> **Instrumental good** A good that is good for a particular purpose

According to Hick:
- We are made in God's image, but must develop into his likeness (the spiritual aspect of humans).
- In this vale of soul-making, we have to try to come to a fuller knowledge of God (overcoming the epistemic distance).
- We can only do this with free will; if God presented himself to us, we would not be able to choose a relationship with God with complete freedom. In the same way, true love has to be freely chosen: we cannot be forced to love someone.
- We need to use evil and suffering in this process, by responding appropriately to them.
- Our response to suffering develops our virtues, such as compassion and charity, which helps us to grow as people.

Hick felt that the idea of hell contributes to the problem of evil, because no good can come out of a place of eternal suffering. For Hick, hell must be a place of cleansing – further soul-making – before humans go on to heaven, especially as people die at different stages of their soul-making process and some die as a result of innocent suffering. Hick therefore believes in **universal salvation**, which, for some, will take place after further opportunities to develop into the likeness of God.

Strengths

- Hick's approach seems to overcome many of the weaknesses in the Augustinian theodicy. Evil is a tool used by God, and not a result of God failing to anticipate the results of free will; it also does not rely on seminal presence to justify its approach.
- Its developmental aspect is in line with modern understandings of evolution.
- It allows a non-literal approach to *Genesis*.
- It incorporates suffering, a very real thing that people experience, into its approach.
- It looks beyond the moment of suffering and sees a bigger picture.
- It recognises the role of Jesus in Christian thought as not just a role model but also the reason all may go to heaven.
- It places relationships at the centre of human existence – with God and also with each other – which corresponds to how we experience life.
- It recognises that true virtues do not simply get given to someone – they must be developed.
- Universal salvation seems closer to an understanding of a God who loves and cares for his whole creation.
- It gives a purpose to natural evil that other theodicies find difficult to explain.

Weaknesses

- Why is the epistemic gap so great and why is the world so full of suffering? Why couldn't the world have been a little bit nicer?
- Hick's approach does not take into account the suffering of animals or of the planet. Some would say that this suffering is of a far greater scale and therefore more important than human suffering; the only difference is that we can communicate our pain clearly to each other; all of God's creation has importance.
- Some question why God could not have created a world where humans always make the right choices. It would not be necessary for us to be aware that this is how the world was created.
- Hick does not explain the imbalance of suffering in the world between different people, nor the sheer quantity of innocent suffering; all he suggests is that the end goal in heaven must be worth it.
- If you knew that whatever you did you would get the grade you want in the summer exams, it is likely you wouldn't be reading this book – in the same way, universal salvation seems to remove some of the freedom that Hick keeps central.
- Universal salvation also seems to undermine what Jesus achieved through dying and rising, and reduces him to a role model, which makes some Christians doubt the truth of the theodicy.
- Surely there are ways other than pain, suffering and evil, for God to develop humanity? Why would a perfect God use evil as a means to an end?
- Some people, such as babies or those with disabilities, are unable to use suffering in a developmental way – is it fair for them to suffer at all?

Key word

Universal salvation The idea that everyone goes to heaven

Typical mistake

Hick's theodicy is sometimes dismissed too quickly because universal salvation seems unfair – ensure you can show you understand the whole theodicy.

Revision activity

Some of the strengths correspond to some of the weaknesses and could in an exam be put in the same paragraph to increase your analysis and evaluation mark.

Making links

Hick's views on the afterlife and salvation are studied in the Developments in Christian Thought book.

Now test yourself

7 According to Hick, humans are created in God's image but must develop into what?
8 What did Hick mean by saying the world is a vale of soul-making?

TESTED ☐

6.5 Discussing the problem of evil

Analysing the logical and evidential approaches

The logical problem of evil does contain some assumptions.

- The definition of an all-powerful God assumes that God's power means that God can do absolutely anything, but it might be that God's power is limited because God has given humans free will.
- The idea of an all-loving God assumes that our understanding of love is correct – Hick sees suffering as developmental, so in his view God must be more benevolent by allowing suffering.
- The idea that evil exists is, of course, challenged by Augustine, who says that evil is simply a privation. Irenaean theodicies do not deny that evil exists, but argue that its existence is not set against omnipotence and (omni)benevolence.

The evidential problem of evil argues that the observation we have of evil in the world is enough to argue against the existence of God. These arguments assume that we know fully what it is to be God and what it is to make God's decisions. Religious believers might think this is the wrong starting point and reject this whole approach.

Augustine: is God spared the blame?

Do the Fall of angels and humans and the understanding of privation remove the blame for evil from God?

Yes (God is spared the blame)	No (God still is partially or fully to blame)
Privation means that evil is not something that God can have made	Evil seems to be more significant than a 'privation'
Natural evil came about by the disruption to the order of God's creation	God could still stop, prevent or change natural evils – or protect the victims
Moral evil comes about by continued use of free will	God does not have to hold us accountable for the sins of Adam and Eve
The focus is God's refusal to engage with evil – God keeps away from it	God does not *have* to keep away from it – that is not the sign of a loving creator

Hick: does soul-making justify evil?

Hick's theory does not fully explore the issue of balance and quantity of suffering nor fully take into account other sufferings in the world, such as animal sufferings – it is very much centred on humans. Although Hick would point to universal salvation as a way of justifying the sufferings of the world, arguably, if we know we are all going to go to heaven, perhaps our freedom is not genuine as we cannot choose to be bad in the same way; presumably true freedom requires the genuine option of us ending up in hell.

Religious believers might feel that suffering does improve people in the long term and that it allows them to put their trust in God and accept what is happening to them. Christians would point to the suffering of Jesus as the model for their suffering. It is perhaps an assumption to say that suffering is intrinsically bad (bad in and of itself) – it could be instrumentally good (good because it helps towards a good end).

Making links

Further definitions of God's power and love are discussed in Chapter 7, The nature or attributes of God.

Exam tip

A question that asks whether monotheism can be defended in the face of evil would require you to consider evidence for the existence of God, as well as whether evil can be justified even if the specific theodicies studied are rejected.

Now test yourself

9 What might a Christian say is the ultimate example of suffering?

TESTED

Exam checklist

- Explain and compare the logical and evidential presentations of the problem of evil.
- Explain how Augustine uses the Fall to explain moral and natural evil.
- Explain how Hick adapts Irenaean theodicies to explain the purpose of suffering.
- Evaluate whether Augustine has sufficiently spared God from blame for evil.
- Analyse whether the idea of a 'vale of soul-making' can justify the extent of evils.
- Critically assess whether it is possible to defend monotheism in the face of evil.

Exam tip

It is important to make sure that in your analysis of a topic you are always being fair to the view you are considering. The sample below examines two different approaches to analysing Augustine.

Sample work

First attempt	Improvement
Augustine said that evil came about because of Original Sin at the Fall of Adam and Eve. When Adam and Eve disobeyed God in the Garden of Eden, they created disharmony in the world. However, as the *Genesis* story has been shown to be false, Augustine's theodicy fails.	Some would criticise Augustine's view of disharmony in the world coming through Original Sin and the Fall of Adam and Eve because the *Genesis* story may not be literally true. Augustine said that when Adam and Eve disobeyed God, their punishment illustrates how the perfect relationship between God and the world was broken. The *Genesis* story might be rejected on the evidence of evolution, for example. However, if the story is taken to be symbolically true, it might be argued that Augustine's theodicy can still teach people today about the reasons for suffering.

Going further: Irenaeus

As we saw, Hick adapted Irenaeus' theodicy from the second century. It is useful to know some more detail about Irenaeus' original approach.

According to Irenaeus:
- God created humans in his image and we need to develop into his likeness.
- This development is like a child needing to start on their mother's milk before moving on to solid foods.
- Our development uses suffering to learn, just like Jonah learnt when he was in the belly of the whale.
- God is like a potter, moulding his clay. Just like clay needs to be moist to be moulded, we need to keep ourselves moist by being open to his workmanship. If we do we will be highly rewarded.
- If we do not then we will be condemned to hell, which is a very real possible outcome for Irenaeus.

7 The nature or attributes of God

7.1 Introduction

This chapter is about what people fundamentally mean when they use the word 'God'. God's nature is described with some common adjectives, such as omnipotent, benevolent and so on, but it is how these different descriptions work together that gives the best understanding of 'God'. The task of the philosopher of religion is to decide which model of God he or she wants to follow – how to understand each of the **attributes** alone and in combination. Behind the whole process for the religious believer is the question of whether God remains 'worthy of worship'.

Some of the key thinkers covered in this chapter are:
- Boethius, a Roman philosopher (480–524)
- Anselm, Archbishop of Canterbury and monk (1033–1109)
- Aquinas, a medieval philosopher (1224–1274)
- Descartes, often called the father of western philosophy (1596–1650)
- Swinburne, a modern philosopher (1934–).

> **Key word**
>
> **Attribute** A quality or descriptor

> **Revision activity**
>
> The chapter considers the attributes of God from the specification by theme. It is an interesting exercise to consider them by scholar. Boethius, Anselm and Swinburne are mentioned on the specification; you might have studied others in class. Go through the chapter building notes on each of the individuals and explore their model of God.

The specification says

Topic	Content	Key knowledge
The nature or attributes of God	Developments in the understanding of:	
	● omnipotence	● divine power and self-imposed limitation
	● omniscience	● divine knowledge and its interaction with temporal existence and free will
	● (omni)benevolence	● divine benevolence and just judgement of human actions, including Boethius's argument relating this to divine foreknowledge, eternity and free will
	● eternity	● divine eternity and divine action in time, including Anselm's four-dimensionalist approach as an extension of Boethius's view
	● free will	● the extent to which human free will reasonably coexists with these attributes ● the above should be studied with reference to alternative possibilities presented by Boethius, Anselm and Swinburne
Learners should have the opportunity to study developments in the understanding of the nature of God and the different possibilities presented by the key thinkers, including: ● whether or not it is possible, or necessary, to resolve the apparent conflicts between divine attributes ● whether Boethius, Anselm or Swinburne provides the most useful understanding of the relationship between divinity and time ● whether or not any of these thinkers are successful in resolving the problems of divine knowledge, benevolence, justice, eternity and human free will ● whether the attributes should be understood as subject to the limits of logical possibility or of divine self-limitation.		

7.2 Omnipotence

Omnipotence is the idea that God can do anything. However, the debate in this section lies in what it means to say he can 'do anything'.

Key words

Omnipotence All-powerful

Arbitrary Random

God can do anything, including the impossible

The idea that God can do the logically impossible means that God can make a square circle or make 2 + 2 = 5. As all logic comes from God, God can change logic or suspend it for a time. Scholars such as Descartes take this approach: if omnipotence does not mean that God can do absolutely anything, how could he perform miracles or save the world through Jesus? We may not understand how God could be like this, but we have limited reason. Anselm's view was that omnipotence means that God has unlimited power and so God could even have the power to lie – but he won't because of his benevolence; having this power is not easy for God!

● This view might make God into an **arbitrary** figure who becomes unpredictable.
● This might make someone question why God does not change the laws so that we do not do evil.
● The Bible says that God cannot lie.

God can do only the logically possible

Aquinas argued that God can only do what is possible and which does not lead to a contradiction and thus cannot create a square circle because a square circle cannot exist. His view was that logical possibility means that God can only do what a perfect God can do – that is, he cannot sin. It cannot be right to say God could sin because that is not a part of his logical nature. Aquinas also argues that God cannot change the past.

Swinburne agrees and argues that God being able to do everything has to be understood in context. A square circle is not 'a thing' and so God cannot create one; so, to say God can do every 'thing' does not limit him because it only refers to logically possible powers.

> **Key quote**
>
> Some things were in the realm of the merely possible when they remained yet to be done, but now when they have been done they have ceased to be possible.
>
> Aquinas, *Summa Theologica*

Self-imposed limitation

It has been suggested that perhaps, in creating a limited universe, God decided that he would only operate within the natural laws he created, thus self-imposing a limitation on his power. If the universe is carefully fine-tuned then any undue interference from God would upset the balance of the universe. For Christians, this would make sense of God limiting himself by becoming a human in Jesus Christ. It would also tie in with the Biblical presentation of God's power as far surpassing human understanding without being unlimited: the emphasis is more on God's power over the universe rather than the power to do anything. Some thinkers use the word 'almighty' instead of all-powerful to describe God in this context.

● In this approach, is God still worthy of worship if he has specifically chosen to allow the extent of suffering that there is in the world, or if he has chosen to allow some but not all potential miracles?

Now test yourself

1 Who might say that God could make 3 × 3 = 11?
2 Which two philosophers say that God can only do what is logically possible for a perfect God to do?
3 Which approach to omnipotence is perhaps most in line with the Bible's presentation of God?

7.3 Eternity

There are two approaches to God and time. The first, and traditional, view held by Boethius, Anselm and Aquinas is that God is **eternal** because God created time and is outside time. The second is that God moves along the timeline as we do – God is **everlasting**. This is the view held by Swinburne, among others.

God as eternal

In this approach, God can perfectly see the past, present and future – this means that God's knowledge and power are not limited. God created the universe and is apart from the universe in terms of both space and time.

Boethius's view takes into account the problem that if God is eternal and knows the future, how can we be morally responsible for our actions? He begins with his understanding of eternity:

- To understand knowledge, Boethius says that we have to understand the nature of the knower.
- What does it mean, therefore, to consider God as eternal? This will help us to understand his nature.
- Eternity is the 'simultaneous possession of boundless life' – God possesses all at the same time all of existence (boundless life).
- This is 'made clearer by comparison with temporal things' – it is better understood when we compare God's nature with our natures.
- We do not have boundless life and so we live from moment to moment – from past to present to future. We do not 'embrace the infinity of life all at once'.
- However, God does and so God cannot have lost the past and doesn't have the future to look forward to. God is always infinitely present to himself.
- Eternity, for Boethius, therefore, is something that God holds all in one go. Time has no meaning for God – everything is the present for God. This means that for God, 'now' is the creation of the world, the coming of Jesus, the Battle of Hastings, me writing this book, you reading it and my great-great-great-grandchild being born: all of this is the present, at the same time.

Anselm continued this approach and from it developed his four-dimensionalist approach.

- From God's perspective, he rejects the idea that the only aspect of time that exists is the present (the past has gone; the future has not yet happened): this is how humans live. We are within space and within time.
- God, however, is separate to time in the same way that he is separate to space.
- The past, present and future all exist as terms that are relative to each other, just like we relate to each other in terms of space (using phrases such as 'in front of me').
- Time is a dimension, just like length, breadth and height are the three dimensions of space.
- We might be limited by both space and time, but God is not limited by either.
- In the same way that God is present every*where*, God is present every*when*.
- Anselm develops Boethius's idea of the simultaneous present by stating that the 'eternal present' is different to our idea of the present and eternity becomes a non-temporal word – it becomes a word to do with the fourth dimension, alongside the dimensions of space.

Key words

Eternal Separate to time; timeless

Everlasting Within the timeline; from beginning to end

Revision activity

Try to analyse the similarities and differences between Boethius and Anselm by writing their views in a table.

Key quote

[C]onsider temporal things: whatever lives in time lives only in the present, which passes from the past into the future, and no temporal thing has such a nature that it can simultaneously embrace its entire existence, for it has not yet arrived at tomorrow and no longer exists in yesterday.

Boethius, *The Consolation of Philosophy*

God as everlasting

Many modern philosophers reject the idea of God as eternal as being an idea that has been inherited from Greek philosophers which has never been fully challenged.

Swinburne's starting point is that the God of the Bible seems to be within time: God takes part on the battlefields with the Israelites, he changes his mind and he is constantly interacting with people through the New Testament. He rejects the idea of the 'simultaneous present' because he does not think it is coherent for God to view two events at different times at one timeless moment and he argues that it is difficult for a timeless God to be said to be doing a miracle at a specific time or to say that God became a human at a particular point in history.

A common example is that of Hezekiah in the Old Testament. Hezekiah is told that God intends for him to die but he prays to God and God hears his prayer and sees that he is upset to die and God decides that he will extend Hezekiah's life.

For Swinburne, the eternal, unchanging God needs to be rejected because this is not a God that can have relationships with humans and relationships are at the centre of human existence and the way the world has been ordered. A God who is eternal cannot love his creation in the way that a God who is everlasting can.

Analysing the approaches

The idea that God is eternal creates questions for the religious believer:
- How can a God who is so separate to the world have a relationship with those in it – or indeed intervene in it? Is there any point in praying for things?
- If God is eternal and knows the future, are we free to choose what our futures will look like?
- If God knows the future, surely he is responsible for the problem of evil?
- If God is both eternal and knows the future can we be held morally responsible for our actions? Are we truly free?
- Is it a play on words to say that things work differently for God?
- If God is eternal, can God choose between one course of action and another? Does God need to?

Equally, there are questions arising from the idea of God being everlasting:
- Has God been limited too much? Can God be omniscient or omnipotent if he is within time?
- If God does not know what choices we will make, is he still worthy of our worship?
- Should we trust the Bible's account of God when the Bible might simply be a human text?
- Did God exist before time? If not, has time always existed and is it logical that time existed before the universe?
- If God is everlasting, God changes with time. Can a perfect God change?

Exam tip

A useful sentence starter for essays on this topic is, 'If eternity is taken to mean that God is timeless …'. Similar phrases can be used for the other attributes.

Key quote

I have heard your prayer and seen your tears; I will add fifteen years to your life.

Isaiah, 38:5

Now test yourself

4 According to Boethius, what must we understand in order to understand knowledge and eternity?
5 According to Anselm, what are the four dimensions that should be considered alongside each other?
6 What is Swinburne's main evidence for saying that God is primarily portrayed as everlasting?

TESTED ☐

7.4 Omniscience

REVISED

Divine knowledge and its interaction with temporal existence

God's knowledge is clearly not the same as our knowledge. Apart from anything else, we are confined to a particular place at any one time and God is not: I do not know what my co-author is doing at the moment I type this, but God can know this. God's knowledge goes beyond this, however, as God knows events from the past that have not been recorded and have been forgotten and God always knows what is morally right to do.

A key question is whether God can know the future, because if God does know the future, why does he not prevent future bad things from happening? Equally, if God chooses not to prevent these things from happening, are we really responsible morally for our wrong actions? We began to explore these in the last section.

In many ways, **omniscience** can fall into similar categories to omnipotence. If God can know absolutely everything then the idea of middle knowledge might be explored. This is the view that God knows not only everything that happens in the past, present or future, but God also knows everything that might have happened if other choices had been made. This seems vast, but it is only as vast as anything to do with the infinity of God. Many have questioned whether it is necessary even to discuss the issue, but others suggest that in order for God to know the future, he must know the process of thoughts and decisions that lead to it.

Timeless God is often portrayed as being like a man standing on a mountain, looking at a road and seeing all the points on that road at once. This illustrates how God can know the past, present and future, but also raises the question of how God can intervene in time.

If omniscience is the idea that God can know all that it is logically possible to know, then it could be argued that God does not logically have to know the future and an everlasting model of God would be coherent.

- God could be seen as being like a chess Grand Master playing a game against a novice (as modern philosopher Peter Geach suggested). The novice is free to make moves according to his or her own skill level, but ultimately the Grand Master is in control.
- In the same way, God could be seen to be in control and, whatever choices we make according to our own natures (skill levels), God's plan can still win through.
- The idea of God having a plan and guiding people along it is, of course, very much in line with the Biblical view of God.

Schleiermacher said that God's knowledge of us is like the knowledge of a very close friend. As God knows us incredibly well, he can accurately predict what we will do, although we still remain free to choose to do otherwise. This brings us back to the central issue in this topic about free will. Can we say that we are free if God knows the future?

Divine knowledge and its interaction with free will

Boethius continued the argument started in the previous section to explore fully the nature of God's knowledge and how it relates to our knowledge and how we can still claim to be free beings.

Key word

Omniscience All-knowing

Making links

The nature of knowledge is discussed in the Developments in Christian Thought book, Chapter 3.

Key quote

Now although contingent events come into actual existence successively, God does not, as we do, know them in their actual existence successively, but all at once; because his knowledge is measured by eternity, as is also his existence; and eternity, which exists as a simultaneous whole, takes in the whole of time.

Aquinas, *Summa Theologica*

Revision activity

Check you can see how Boethius and Anselm's logic carries through from the section on eternal God.

- As God exists with time as a simultaneous present, God's knowledge of what we call the past, present and future is seen in one single vision – as if things were occurring in a single instant.
- Therefore, God does not know the future, but knows the simultaneous, unchanging present.
- The fact that God knows something in advance does not mean that God changes the nature of this thing: God simply sees things that are future for us as present for him.
- Boethius distinguishes between 'simple' and 'conditional' necessity:
  - Something is classed as 'simple necessity' if it 'just is' – 'humans are necessarily mortal'.
  - Something has 'conditional necessity' if it has a condition added to it – 'as long as someone is walking then his feet are moving him forward'.
- Therefore, when God sees something in our future, he is seeing it as necessary, but 'conditionally necessary' because God sees it under the condition that it has been freely chosen by a human.
- Boethius concludes that we remain entirely free because we are completely separate from God's foreknowledge.

Anselm's four-dimensionalist approach expands on Boethius's approach and concludes the following about free will:

- As God is separate from time and space and as God experiences eternity as a dimension, rather than in terms of time, our free will is preserved.
- God can see us in our past, present and future and he can see us making free decisions.
- As the future for God is not a matter of time, but it is a matter of time for us, the future is unchanging for God, but changing for us.

Swinburne's everlasting model of God, of course, means that God does not know the future because God is alongside us on the timeline. He may be able to predict it very accurately, but the knowledge is not fixed until it happens.

Analysing the approaches

Boethius's approach seems successfully to separate our knowledge from God's, but it raises a number of issues which perhaps Anselm overcomes:

- It is difficult to understand how God can act within this understanding of time and knowledge – and if God cannot intervene in the world, miracles are rejected, as is the divine nature of Jesus Christ. Anselm's approach perhaps improves this problem as it changes the understanding of eternity, but still leaves God very separate from the world. It is possible to argue that God, being unique, should not be considered in human terms.
- A number of scholars reject as incoherent Boethius's idea of God being simultaneously present because it makes no sense to talk of the past, present and future all being in the present; again, Anselm's approach might begin to overcome this. However, it also helps to consider the fact that if God is timeless, he must be separate to his creation.

> **Key quote**
>
> That which he foreknows in his eternity is immutable, in time it is mutable before it happens.
>
> Anselm, *De Concoria*

> **Typical mistake**
>
> Candidates sometimes let themselves down because they only select aspects of Boethius (or another named scholar) to explain, rather than exploring the argument as a whole.

Now test yourself

TESTED

7 Who spoke of God as: (a) a chess Grand Master; (b) a very close friend?
8 What two types of necessity does Boethius talk about?
9 Who said that for us the future is changing, but for God it is not?

7.5 (Omni)benevolence

God's **benevolence** suggests that God's entire attitude is one of compassion, love, and fairness – like a constant and active force. It is not just about the human word 'love'. God's omnibenevolence is relational, total, linked to justice and judgement – it is fair, holy, and expected to be found in his followers.

In the Bible, the words used are the Hebrew word *hesed* (Old Testament) and the Greek word *agape* (New Testament) and both words are about a total disposition in a person towards kindness, compassion and fairness to others, reflected in how God 'feels' about the world. Jesus' focus on *agape* leads Christians to understand it in the context of loving even enemies, as well as the central idea of forgiveness.

Christians believe God's benevolence has been shown to the world through: creation; interventions: miracles and especially the incarnation of Jesus; answered prayers; and the guidance given to the world, especially the commandments and the **covenant**.

Aquinas argued that justice is about God doing the right thing, even if punishment is involved. Certainly, many Christians have had no issue in arguing that God condemns some to hell and even predestines some to hell before they are born.

Issues arising

Linking benevolence with the other attributes led Boethius and Anselm to conclude that God's foreknowledge is separate to human freedom and rewards and punishments are therefore just and fair. Boethius concludes his argument about foreknowledge in *The Consolation of Philosophy* with 'God sees us from above and knows all things in his eternal present and judges our future, free actions, justly distributing rewards and punishments'.

Omnibenevolence raises other core issues:

● Do evil and suffering contradict a benevolent God? Some would argue that it does because God would not allow his people to suffer. Others would argue that justice, fairness and free will mean that God might have to allow suffering, perhaps using some of the theodicies or techniques discussed in Chapter 6.	● What does it mean to call God 'good'? The Euthyphro dilemma is an ancient philosophical conundrum that suggests that either God defines goodness (and so it becomes arbitrary) or God is subject to an independent standard of goodness (and so isn't the highest being) – either way God is not worthy of worship. The dilemma is often felt to be solved by Aquinas' approach that God can only command *out of* his goodness, so, by definition, no commands could be arbitrary.
● Can our language explain fully God's benevolence? Is it presumptuous to claim that we can understand God's nature? Some of the tools described in Chapter 8 might help to explore how we should understand benevolence fully.	● For Christians, faith has the final word. God journeys alongside his people and even if we do not fully understand how the world works, God's revelation assures Christians that somehow God's attributes do work together.
● Is hell the ultimate sign that God does give up on some people or is hell a place, as the Roman Catholic Church argues, that people send *themselves* to?	

Conflicts between divine attributes

Where there are conflicts between the divine attributes, they either need to be resolved using another tool (such as a theodicy) or they suggest that the model of God being used is not quite coherent and needs to be adapted.

- **Omnipotence** could be argued to conflict with benevolence because of the problem of evil. If God is eternal then why does an omnipotent God not stop bad things happening, or why does the God of the Bible seem surprised by events? If God is everlasting, can God still be seen to be omnipotent, or does the understanding of omnipotence need to change?
- **Omniscience**. If God cannot know the future, what does that suggest about God's omnipotence? The biggest conflict is between omniscience and omnibenevolence because it questions what God chooses to do with the knowledge he has.
- **Omnibenevolence** is perhaps the fundamental description of God. Understanding this attribute may lead someone to be able to understand the other core attributes of God and thus resolve any perceived conflicts.

A popular analogy is that God is like a diamond – just like a diamond has many faces, each of which gives a different understanding, so too God can be examined from different directions. Islam lists 99 names of Allah, each of which gives a different perspective on God. However, modern atheist thinkers would reject belief in God in its entirety, challenging the approach of theists:

- as wishful thinking
- as projecting a fear of death or of loneliness
- as trying to stamp human authority onto the earth
- as being examples of lazy thinking, being prepared to believe in something for which there is insufficient evidence.

Limits to the attributes

Whereas Descartes' approach was to say that God can do anything, including the impossible, and therefore not remain consistent, many philosophers place limits on God:

- **Logical possibility**. Aquinas argued that God cannot do the illogical or impossible. Does it matter that God cannot do the impossible or to change his mind and change a law of nature? Many believers would say not.
- **Self-limitation**. Has God in some way limited his power, either by deciding to conform to the laws of nature and logic when he created the universe, or by creating an epistemic distance (see Chapter 6)? Many religious believers suggest that this distance needs to be overcome if we are to have a full relationship with God and that the quest for a human is to be able to do this; others question why God would make humans just for this purpose. Perhaps God is eternal, but in creating space and time he has placed himself on the timeline until the universe ends. Some would accuse the idea of self-limitation as being a play on words and ideas to try to make an idea that doesn't work (i.e. the attributes) fit together.

> **Key quote**
>
> God is greater than all we can say, greater than all that we can know; and not merely does he transcend our language and our knowledge, but he is beyond the comprehension of every mind whatsoever.
>
> Aquinas, *De Divinis Nominibus*

> **Making links**
>
> Non-religious approaches and challenges to Christianity are examined in the Developments in Christian Thought book, especially Chapters 9 and 10.

> **Key quote**
>
> God is himself responsible for there being limits to his knowledge of how we will act.
>
> Swinburne, *Was Jesus God?*

7.7 Comparing Boethius, Anselm and Swinburne

Some key areas to consider are:

- Anselm develops Boethius's views and tries to overcome the possibility that Boethius does not seem to have space for a God who intervenes. He does this by focusing on the idea of time for God being different to time for ourselves; eternity is not a time-word, but a dimension. However, Anselm is still left with God sitting very separately to the universe and this raises questions about how God can interact with it.
- Swinburne takes a different approach and argues that his view of God and time is more in line with the Biblical view. However, this assumes the accuracy of the Biblical view. If the Bible is simply a human account of God's relationship with the world, then it is a human perspective on God, which is already limiting God because human understanding is limited. This might explain why Swinburne seems to limit God to being everlasting, rather than eternal.
- Swinburne's approach does seem to help with issues such as prayer. If it is logical to say that an eternal God is separate to the world, does God know what the date today is? It might not matter, but it does to me if I have an operation on a particular date and I want God to be with me. However, it could be argued that God might not know what the date is *to him* (because that is illogical) but he does know what the date is *to me*, just like I understand that it is 11 a.m. to me now, but 12 noon to someone in Paris now.

> **Key quote**
>
> In my opinion, the timeless view is incompatible with everything else that religious believers have wanted to say about God. For example, it does seem strongly that God being omniscient entails that he hears the prayers of humans at the same time as they utter them; yet on the timeless view God does not exist at the same time as (simultaneously with) any moment in our timescale.
>
> Swinburne, *Was Jesus God?*

- Equally, however, God might not be able to act if he is eternal because doing a miracle for me now will change the past for someone in the year 2500, which, as science fiction shows us so clearly, would create real issues in logic.
- Boethius's starting point is important: we need to understand that God sees things differently to us.
- This can even help with understanding how Swinburne would approach the issue of free will and omniscience. Although for Swinburne, God is everlasting, he is able to know all that it is logically possible for God to know. God might know everything about us as individuals and because God cannot be wrong, God will successfully predict how we will respond in any situation. It could be argued that saying God is everlasting does not necessarily limit him that much.
- Our free will might also be affected by genes, upbringing, psychological factors, our conditioning and so on; we may not even be free ourselves.

> **Revision activity**
>
> Bring together the strengths and weaknesses of each of the divine attributes in Sections 7.2 to 7.5 and decide which apply to each of Boethius, Anselm and Swinburne's views.

> **Exam tip**
>
> Use this material alongside your notes from class and your text books to be clear about each of the issues. Success in the exam comes from being able to discuss the issues as if you've done so before!

Exam checklist

- Explain different approaches to God's omnipotence.
- Explain different approaches to God's (omni)benevolence.
- Explain different approaches to God's omniscience.
- Explain different approaches to God's relationship with time.
- Explain how free will coexists with other attributes of God.
- Compare Boethius's views on divine foreknowledge with Anselm's four-dimensionalist approach.
- Evaluate whether Swinburne's approach successfully overcomes issues in traditional philosophy.
- Assess whether a God who knows the future can have created free humans.
- Evaluate whether God's attributes can be said to be limited by logical possibility or divine self-limitation.

Sample work

This chapter has explored some fundamental aspects of the philosophy of religion in quite some depth and there is a lot of overlap between different parts. Essays in this area often suffer from candidates trying to do too much, rather than simply focusing on the question. The following table imagines an essay on omnipotence and what part of its plan might look like. The first attempt would not lead to an essay that fully explored omnipotence.

First attempt	Improvement
Omnipotence. Logically impossible (Descartes)	*Option 1* God can do the logically impossible. What this says about God's nature and being arbitrary
Logically possible (Aquinas). Link to eternal God and Boethius	*Option 2* God can do only the logically possible. Is there evidence in the world of this God? (Problem of evil)
Self-limited. Link to other attributes – Swinburne – God is everlasting	*Option 3* God is self-limited. Does this make God worthy of worship?

Going further: Other attributes

The specification lists four key attributes of God, but many other lists exist. Some others that you might research more or use in writing are listed below with some areas to consider. As with all the others in this topic, some might be rejected or defined differently by different believers.

Attribute	Meaning	Example areas to consider
Personal	God desires a relationship with his people	Can we have a relationship with a God outside time? What evidence is there of God wanting a personal relationship with people?
Transcendent	God is separate to time and space	How can this God intervene in the world? How can we worship a God we cannot have proper access to?
Immanent	God is within space and time	How can this God be great enough to be worshipped?
Immutable	God cannot change	How can a God who cannot change respond to our prayers?
Impassible	God cannot feel anything	How can this be a comfort to those who suffer?
Simple	God cannot be divided into parts – physically or in terms of his other attributes	How useful is it to consider the different attributes separately?

8 Religious language

8.1 Introduction

REVISED

One of the key debates in religious language is the question of how words can be used to adequately express ideas about God. In order to understand this, think of the difficulty of describing something such as falling in love or going to a concert if the listener has not experienced it. Our words may not be able to fully do justice to the experience. This problem is magnified when it comes to describing God. God is by definition beyond our limited human comprehension and experience. How can words be of use in helping us to understand God? The first of our approaches to religious language, the *via negativa*, accepts this problem and suggests that the solution is to avoid making positive statements about God; we are only able to describe what God is not. The second approach to language, the *via positiva*, by analogy, suggests that words used of God and words used in everyday life do have a connection. Aquinas argues that they are 'like' their everyday meaning but not the same. The final approach to religious language is to treat all words about God symbolically; words used to describe God are not literally true.

Key words

Cognitive Statements about God that can be known to be either true or false

Non-cognitive Statements about God are not subject to truth or falsity

Univocal The idea that words have the same meaning at all times

Equivocal The idea that the same word is used with two completely different meanings

The specification says

Topic	Content	Key knowledge
Religious language: negative, analogical or symbolic	Apophatic way – the *via negativa*	● the argument that theological language is best approached by negation
	Cataphatic way – the *via positiva*	● the understanding of religious language in terms of analogy, with reference to: – Aquinas's analogy of attribution and analogy of proper proportion
	Symbol	● understanding of the language of religious expression in terms of symbol, with reference to: – Tillich's view of theological language as almost entirely symbolic
	Learners should have the opportunity to discuss issues related to different views of religious language, including: ● comparison of the usefulness of the above approaches to religious language ● whether or not the apophatic way enables effective understanding of theological discussion ● whether or not Aquinas' analogical approaches support effective expression of language about God ● whether or not religious discourse is comprehensible if religious language is understood as symbolic.	

Each of the approaches to speaking about God claim that religious statements are to some extent **cognitive** as opposed to **non-cognitive** (see Chapter 9 for more on these terms). However, when words are used to describe God, do they mean exactly the same as they would mean in their normal context? This would be to use the words **univocally**. Or do they mean something very different when describing God? This would be to use the words **equivocally**.

Now test yourself

1 What does univocal mean?
2 What does equivocal mean?

TESTED

8.2 Explaining the apophatic way (*via negativa*)

The **apophatic way** or *via negativa* claims that because words are unable to adequately describe God, the only possible statements that can be made are negative statements; statements about what God is not.

God as 'beyond description'

God is beyond our ability to describe. Just as in Judaism where the name of God is not uttered, and in Islam where picturing God is forbidden, the *via negativa* is aware that the danger of using human language of God is that we will imagine or picture our human version of the word we use. When we say that 'God is Good' we cannot help but understand the word 'good' in terms of human goodness. Yet God is not 'good' in this sense, his goodness is beyond our comprehension. The same is true of all God's attributes.

All words when applied to God are equivocal.

The apophatic way – key thinkers

Initially, the apophatic way (*via negativa*) came from Platonic philosophers who realised that the form of the Good was beyond description.

The fifth-century Christian writer Pseudo-Dionysius believed that God was beyond assertion. He was also influenced by Plato and was aware of the limits of our senses as well as our language. To try to make positive statements about God would be to risk an **anthropomorphic** idea of God. Hence only negative terms can preserve the mystery and 'otherness' of God.

The Jewish philosopher Moses Maimonides (1135–1204) argued for the use of the *via negativa* in his *Guide for the Perplexed*. The only positive statement that can be made about God is that he exists. All other descriptions of God must be negative so as to ensure that we are not being improper or disrespectful. He argues that the negative can bring us some knowledge of God. He uses the example of a ship. If we say that the ship is not an accident, not a mineral, not a plant, not a natural body, etc., then he argues that by the tenth statement we will have some knowledge of what a ship is. In the same way, the via negativa allows us to gain some knowledge of God.

> **Key words**
>
> **Apophatic way (*via negativa*)** The idea that the only way of speaking about God and religious ideas is through negative terms, what God is not
>
> **Anthropomorphic** The tendency to describe something in human terms

> **Key quote**
>
> God is beyond all meaning and intelligence, and he alone possesses immortality. His light is called darkness because of its excellence, as no creature can comprehend either what or how it is.
>
> John Scotus Eriugena: Homily on the Prologue to the Gospel of St. John

Now test yourself

3 Why do some thinkers argue that only the apophatic way should be used to speak of God?

8.3 The apophatic way assessed

Key strengths of the apophatic way

- Any language that is used of God is inevitably pictured by its hearers in human terms. This reduces God to a human level. The apophatic way prevents anthropomorphic representations of God.
- Following from this, it can be argued that the apophatic way is hence more respectful in its approach. It recognises that God is transcendent and wholly other to the human realm.
- This approach fits with how religious experiences are perceived by those who experience them, particularly in mysticism. As William James observes (see Chapter 5), religious experiences are ineffable; they cannot be described in ordinary language.

Key weaknesses of the apophatic way

- Even if the apophatic way does give some knowledge of God, it is incredibly limited in what can be known. It is not clear from Maimonides' example (see previous section) that a ship can be described in the way he maintains. It is even less likely that this method can bring any knowledge of God.
- The apophatic way is not a true reflection of how religious believers speak or think about God. The scriptures of all major faiths describe God in positive terms.
- The apophatic way means that the believer has no means of communicating with the non-believer about the subject of God.
- W.R. Inge (1860–1954), Dean of St Paul's Cathedral, argued that denying any description to God leads to an annihilation of God where we potentially lose the connection between God and the world. Flew's argument on falsification would seem to support this view (see Chapter 9). The idea of a God who is not visible, is intangible, etc., seems to bear very little difference to there being no God at all.

> ### Exam tip
>
> In order to access the higher levels on the mark scheme, particularly for AO2, you will need to discuss points raised not just state them. It is important to develop arguments and not just list strengths and weaknesses. See the example below.

Developing arguments on the apophatic way

Proposed difficulty of the *via negativa*	Response and conclusion
The *via negativa* gives very limited knowledge of God. First, it may be a matter of debate which attributes we wish to claim that God is not. It is said that 'God is not evil' and 'God is not weak'. Equally we could say 'God is not green' or 'God is not a cat'. In addition to this, even if we do agree on the attributes, it seems that little is actually being said. There are many things that could be described as not evil and not weak.	This suggests that in order to gain knowledge of God we would need to use an alternative model such as analogy. This would enable us to make statements about God cautiously and positively. However, in doing so, it is important to preserve the insight given to us by the *via negativa* that God is fundamentally beyond description and any language used to describe him is used cautiously.

8.4 The cataphatic way (*via positiva*) – Aquinas and analogy

REVISED

The **cataphatic way** or the *via positiva*, unlike the apophatic way, argues that positive statements can be made about God. Aquinas' theory of **analogy**, which is an example of the *via positiva*, sits between univocal and equivocal theories of language.

Univocal language	Analogy	Equivocal language
Words when applied to God have the same meaning that they have in their normal context. Therefore, risks making God sound human	Words when applied to God have a partial resemblance to their normal use	Words when applied to God have a completely different meaning from their normal use. Therefore, no knowledge of God

We use analogies in everyday speech to help people to understand something they are unfamiliar with, by comparing it to something they are familiar with. For example, we might explain to a younger student that revising for A-levels is like revising for GCSEs, but is harder and requires more time. Likewise when describing God's goodness, it is like human goodness but at a greater level.

Aquinas on analogy

Thomas Aquinas argues that language applied to God is not literal but is analogical. He understands this as happening in two ways.

1 **The analogy of attribution**. The words that we apply to human beings are related to how words are applied to God because there is a causal relationship between the two sets of qualities. Our qualities such as love and wisdom are reflections of those qualities of God. Aquinas uses an interesting example to illustrate this. In medieval times, it was believed that if a creature's urine was healthy then the creature that produced the urine must also be healthy; so 'if the urine is good, then the bull is good'. The bull after all is the cause of the urine! Likewise, by examining human love, wisdom or power we may see a pale reflection of those divine attributes.

2 **The analogy of proper proportion**. The extent to which a being can be said to have certain properties is in proportion to the type of being we are describing. To say that a 10-year-old is a good footballer is different to saying that an England international is a good footballer. When we say that a human is 'good' we are speaking of a finite being. When describing God, we are speaking of an infinite being so the 'goodness' is in proportion to that.

John Hick on analogy

John Hick (see Chapter 6, The problem of evil) develops Aquinas' example of analogy of proper proportion using the example of the term 'faithfulness'. Just as we might see a dog's faithfulness as smaller or more limited than human faithfulness (although it is possible to debate this), so too our faithfulness is vastly smaller when compared to the faithfulness of God.

Key words

Cataphatic way (*via positiva*) The idea that God can be spoken of in positive terms

Analogy A comparison between two things in order to help us understand the less familiar thing

Now test yourself

4 Which of the ideas of analogy makes use of the causal link between God and humans? Is it analogy of attribution or analogy of proportion?
5 Hick develops Aquinas' idea of analogy of _____.

TESTED

8.5 The cataphatic way (*via positiva*) assessed

There are a number of strengths and weaknesses of the idea of analogy.

Strengths of the cataphatic way (*via positiva*)

- The theory manages to avoid two of the key errors that theories in religious language can make. It is not univocal so avoids speaking anthropomorphically of God. It is not equivocal so avoids the **agnosticism** that comes with this approach.
- The method of analogy which invites us to describe God in visual terms is not dissimilar to the method that Jesus used in describing the Kingdom of God. He taught in parables that began with the phrase 'the Kingdom of God is like…'
- Aquinas may be right to argue that if language cannot be used at all of God then we are not able to do theology or philosophy as discussion relies on words having at least some positive meaning.

> **Key word**
>
> **Agnosticism** The idea that God's nature and existence cannot be known

Weaknesses of the cataphatic way (*via positiva*)

- The theory of analogy does allow some picturing in a way that the *via negativa* does not, but with this comes the danger that in 'picturing' an aspect of God we are interpreting on an individual level. 'God is my shepherd' may be imagined and understood differently by different people.
- Linked to this, some critics of analogy are concerned that in order to understand the word that is being applied to God we have to translate that word into univocal language first. Indeed Swinburne has argued that religious statements are not analogical, but are univocal. The meaning remains in contact with the everyday meaning but is stretched.
- It is not always easy to know how far the meaning is stretched. Analogy tells us that 'God is love' is not the same as human love, but is not completely different. How far are we to stretch the meaning? Hence it may be that analogy only provides a little knowledge of God.

Developing arguments on the cataphatic way (*via positiva*)

Proposed strength of analogy	Discussion
Unlike the *via negativa*, analogy is able to provide some knowledge of God and his attributes. The claim that 'God is all good', although it is not a human goodness, at least provides some understanding of God's nature, whereas 'God is not evil' and 'God is not cruel' does not.	However, Catholic theologian Vincent Brummer has challenged this optimistic claim. The idea of analogy gives the appearance of saying something about God but actually it does not. We know that God is not good in a human way but what does it mean to be good in the infinite way that is 'in proportion' to God's being. In response to this, Aquinas might have largely accepted this point – he was well aware that any knowledge of God gained was limited.

Now test yourself

6 Why do some thinkers believe that analogy avoids both agnosticism and anthropomorphism?

8.6 Tillich and symbolic language

Paul Tillich (1886–1965) argues that religious statements are not literally true. Almost all religious language that attempts to express ideas about God is to be understood symbolically.

Typical mistake

You will be familiar with the idea of religious symbols, such as the cross in Christianity or the items on a Passover table in Judaism. Yet it is important to focus your writing on symbolic language. It is not just these objects or events that represent truth; all statements including literal sounding statements such as 'God is Good' are to be understood symbolically according to Tillich.

Signs and symbols

For Tillich, there is a difference between signs and symbols. A sign such as a red traffic light or another road sign points to something. However, a symbol participates in that to which it points. A flag does not merely act as a sign; for many people it represents the nation involved. Likewise the poppy doesn't just point out that people lost their lives; in some way it is part of Remembrance Day and adds to its meaning.

Now test yourself

TESTED

7 According to Tillich, what is the difference between a sign and a symbol?
8 In what ways does symbolic language function like works of art?

Tillich on symbolic language and art

1 We cannot speak literally of God. God is not part of the empirical world and thus can't be represented by literal language. The only statement that can be used of God is that he is the 'Ground of Being' or 'Being itself', the source of everything. All other sentences must be understood symbolically.
2 The symbolic words we ascribe to God cannot be random or invented. Tillich is influenced by Jung in suggesting that they may emerge out of a collective unconscious. Certainly symbols function on an unconscious level as much as a conscious level.
3 Symbols may have a limited lifespan. Just as the Hindu symbol of the swastika has lost its meaning due to Nazi use, so too the words we use to describe God may change over time as some word pictures become more helpful or unhelpful.
4 A symbol opens up levels of reality that would otherwise be closed to us. They also unlock 'hidden depths of our own being'. Tillich draws an analogy here with good works of art. Like art, symbols enable us to grasp deep truths about the world and about ourselves.

Key quote

Every symbol is double edged. It opens up reality, and it opens the soul.

Tillich, *Theology of Culture*

8.7 Symbolic language assessed

Strengths of symbolic language

- It is argued that taking a symbolic view of religious language preserves the transcendence and mystery of God in a way that analogical language does not. To say that God is 'good' has a similar meaning to our everyday use, which is what analogy is saying, risks reducing God to our level. Suggesting that the word 'good' is symbolic seems to avoid this.
- Tillich's insight is that symbols are able to communicate deeply in a way that ordinary language cannot. This insight seems to accurately reflect our sense that the most important things in life are beyond words.
- The idea that symbolic language can be changed with time may in fact be a strength as it ensures that the message remains relevant to its changing cultural context.

Weaknesses of symbolic language

- It is not clear how a symbol participates in that to which it points. To burn a flag or trample on poppies might be seen as an insult but would it really weaken the nation or reduce the importance of the sacrifice of fallen soldiers?
- Tillich's claim that symbolic language is cognitive – providing statements that are true of God – is open to challenge. Some thinkers such as J.H. Randall are happy to accept that religious language is symbolic, but believe that the symbols are non-cognitive and provide no information about God.
- Tillich's idea is that symbols engage us on a deep level in a similar way to how art moves us. Ultimately, this works better for the arts than it does for religion. Tillich is also assuming a connection between religion and the aesthetic.
- If everything participates in 'being itself', it is difficult to see how he can argue that symbols participate in a unique way.
- The fact that symbolic objects and symbolic language are culturally dependent and can change with time may mean that our ideas of God will change over time or be misinterpreted.

Symbolic language discussed

Proposed strength of symbol	Discussion
One possible advantage of the view that language applied to God is symbolic is the idea that symbols are to some extent matters of interpretation. Just as a piece of music may move me in a different way to how it affects my friend, so too symbolic language enables us each to access God in our own way.	However, it is not clear that this is necessarily an advantage. A symbol may mean something to one person, but not the other. Likewise an atheist and a believer may each agree that 'God is all knowing' is a description of the concept of God, yet their view of the sentence is very different. In addition, it is hard to escape the view that the symbols adopted could be arbitrary. The Bible describes God as roaring like a lion, but why not use the idea of 'barks like a dog'. Tillich might answer this latter point by suggesting that symbols have meanings within faith groups, hence there are some interpretations that are beyond what is permitted.

Exam checklist

- Explain and assess the *via negativa* (apophatic way).
- Explain and assess the *via positiva* (cataphatic way), including Aquinas' theory of analogy.
- Explain and assess Tillich's understanding of theological language as symbolic.
- Compare the usefulness of the different approaches to religious language.

Sample work

Critically compare the via negativa with symbolic language as ways of expressing religious beliefs in words. (40 marks)

The question above is a possible question for the A-level paper. By looking carefully at the question above, the following points are worth noting.

1 The focus is the *via negativa* and symbolic language. There is no need to bring analogy or other theories into this.

2 'Compare'. The focus of the question needs to be on drawing out the similarities and differences of the two theories of language.

3 'Critically'. 24 of the 40 marks at A-level are for AO2 – Analysis and evaluation. 'Critically' signals that judgements need to be made as well as just comparisons. Which theory fares better and why?

Typical mistake

It is very easy to glance at exam questions such as the one above, pick out a key word and write pretty much all you know about the topic. Key to writing a good Religious Studies essay is selection of material. This involves making decisions about the material you have learned: what goes in and what stays out.

Going further: Ramsey's view of models and qualifiers

One development of the theory of analogy came from Ian Ramsey (1915–1972) with his theory of models and qualifiers. Just as in ordinary life we may design a model to help us understand something, so too our religious language is a model to help us understand God. These models also have qualifiers with them; these are words that show us how to use the model or specify under what conditions the model might apply.

In the phrase 'Heavenly Father', the word 'father' is a model that helps us to understand the concept of God. The word 'Heavenly' is a qualifier; we must not understand God as an earthly father, he is a very different type of father.

9 Twentieth-century perspectives

9.1 Introduction

If I claim that 'God loves me', what exactly does that mean? Could it be proved or disproved? Is it true or is it a claim that has meaning to me but not to everyone? This topic is related to the previous chapter on religious language and also to the topic of meta-ethics (see the Religion and Ethics section of the specification). This topic involves asking whether statements made about God are **cognitive** or **non-cognitive**. When we make cognitive statements about the world, we are able to establish whether they are true or false using our senses. **Logical positivists** note that this is not the case for religious statements; there is no way to prove that they are true. This leads thinkers such as A.J. Ayer to use the verification principle to argue that religious language is meaningless. The discussion in the falsification symposium starts from a different perspective. Antony Flew asks how, if a religious statement were false, we would be able to establish that it was untrue. R.M. Hare and Basil Mitchell respond to this challenge. Ludwig Wittgenstein suggests that both the verificationists and the falsificationists are looking at the question the wrong way. Religious language is not cognitive and able to be proved or disproved; it is non-cognitive and only has meaning within certain language games. This approach can be contrasted with Aquinas' cognitive approach seen in the previous chapter.

> ### Key words
>
> **Cognitive** Statements about God that can be known to be either true or false
>
> **Non-cognitive** Statements about God are not subject to truth or falsity
>
> **Logical positivism** A movement in philosophy that believed that the aim of philosophers should be to analyse language, particularly the language of science

> ### Now test yourself
>
> 1 Define what is meant by cognitive and non-cognitive statements.
>

The specification says

Topic	Content	Key knowledge
Twentieth-century perspectives and philosophical comparisons	Logical positivism	• the impact of the verification principle on the use of religious language, with reference to: – Ayer's approach to verification
	Wittgenstein's views on language games and forms of life	• how language games may permit religious language to be deemed meaningful yet not cognitive
	Discussion about the factual quality of religious language in the falsification symposium	• the varying arguments, with their associated parables, put forward in relation to theological language by: – Flew, Hare and Mitchell in their contributions to the symposium
	Learners should have the opportunity to discuss issues related to different views of religious language, including: • whether or not any version of the verification principle successfully renders religious language as meaningless • whether or not any participant in the falsification symposium presented a convincing approach to the understanding of religious language • a comparison of the ideas of Aquinas and Wittgenstein, including: – whether a cognitive approach (such as Aquinas' thinking on analogy) or a non-cognitive approach (such as the language games concept of Wittgenstein) present better ways of making sense of religious language – the influence of non-cognitive approaches on the interpretation of religious texts – how far Aquinas' analogical view of theological language remains valuable in philosophy of religion.		

9.2 The verification principle

Supporters of the **verification principle** (verificationists) argued that religious statements are meaningless as they cannot be empirically checked.

Influences on verificationism

The verification principle was influenced by two ideas:

1 **Empiricism**. Thinkers, such as David Hume (1711–1776), suggested two areas of knowledge: a priori knowledge (which he calls Relation of Ideas) and a posteriori knowledge (which he calls Matters of Fact). Hume rejects **metaphysics** including discussion of God as it can be neither of the above.

2 **Focus on language**. Ludwig Wittgenstein (1889–1951) famously said that 'Philosophical problems arise when language goes on holiday' and 'whereof one cannot speak, one must remain silent'. These quotes (although misunderstood by the verificationists) suggested that focusing on language would provide a way forward for philosophers.

The Vienna Circle

The Vienna Circle was a group of philosophers who met in the 1920s and 1930s.

They argued that some statements were meaningful and others were not. In order to identify the difference, they came up with the verification principle. This stated that a statement is only meaningful if it is able to be verified by an actual experience. This means that scientific claims about the world are meaningful, but religious and ethical claims are not.

However ...

As well as religious and ethical statements, this form of the verification principle seems to rule out discussion of a number of areas that cannot be verified. These include historical statements, discussion of scientific laws (we cannot verify that they always apply), and claims about art or beauty.

Ayer's verificationism

A.J. Ayer (1910–1989) accepted the basic idea behind the verification principle. He agreed with Hume and the Vienna Circle that metaphysics should be rejected. Ayer argues that for a statement to be meaningful it must be either a **tautology**, something that is true by definition (known a priori), or something that is verifiable in principle (a posteriori).

It is the verifiable in principle that distinguishes Ayer from the Vienna Circle. We are not required to conclusively prove something by direct observation. We merely have to be able to say how it would be possible to verify it. Ayer uses the example 'there are mountains on the far side of the moon'. which at the time of his writing could not be conclusively verified. Nevertheless, it is a meaningful statement as if we were to orbit the moon we would be able to verify this claim.

> **Key words**
>
> **Verification principle** The belief that statements are only meaningful if they can be verified by the senses. There are strong and weak forms of the principle generally associated with the Vienna Circle and A.J. Ayer, respectively
>
> **Metaphysics** The branch of philosophy dealing with the nature of reality, literally things 'beyond' or 'after' the physical realm
>
> **Tautology** A phrase where the same thing is said twice in different words, e.g. the three-sided triangle

Making links

The logic that leads to ruling out religious statements is the same as that which ruled out moral statements. See Ayer's emotivism in the Religion and Ethics book, Chapter 7.

9.3 Verificationism assessed

Supporting Ayer's verification principle

- Ayer can be seen as offering a significant improvement on the very limited verification principle given by the Vienna Circle. This widens what is meaningful to discussions of historical claims and scientific laws.
- Some philosophers argue that religious and ethical claims are rightly excluded as they are different to other types of statements.
- Ayer also softens the demand for absolute verification of a statement. A statement may not be completely provable, but can be accepted if it could be shown beyond reasonable doubt. This is known as weak verification.

Challenging the verification principle and its conclusions on religion

- The stronger form of verification put forward by the Vienna Circle has been criticised as too rigid. It seems absurd that claims about Julius Caesar coming to Britain might be classed as meaningless.
- It seems that there is agreement in ethics over what is good and to some extent there is agreement by artists regarding what is or isn't beautiful. It is not apparent that ethics and art are meaningless.
- Ayer is not right to rule out all religious statements. Swinburne has noted that some religious claims, e.g. the resurrection of Jesus, would be verifiable if true.
- The verification principle fails its own test. It is self-refuting. The claim that 'statements are only meaningful if they are tautologies or verifiable in principle' is neither a tautology nor verifiable in principle itself! Ayer responded to this challenge by suggesting that the verification principle is not a statement but is a theory. As such it does not need to pass the test.

Hick and eschatological verification

One famous challenge to Ayer's rejection of religious statements comes from John Hick (1922–2012). Hick supports the verification principle but argues that religious claims are verifiable. He uses a parable of two travellers on a road to support this claim. The travellers argue about whether the road leads to the celestial city or whether the road just ends. When they turn the final corner of the road and the celestial city is there, one of them will be proved right. Hick is arguing that religious statements are meaningful eschatologically. At the end of all things, it will be possible to verify God's existence.

Now test yourself

TESTED

2 How does Ayer's verification differ from that of the Vienna Circle?
3 What is eschatological verification?

Key quote

We say that a sentence is factually significant to any given person, if, and only if, he knows ... what observations would lead him, under certain conditions, to accept the proposition as being true, or reject it as being false.

Ayer, *Language, Truth and Logic*

Typical mistake

Note that the Vienna Circle and Ayer are not disproving God's existence. Their challenge to religious language is a more subtle one, that the issue of God is not one that is worthy of serious philosophical discussion.

Exam tip

The argument about the verification principle failing its own test and the response by Ayer is an example of material that would make a good paragraph in an A-level essay. An argument is put; a counterargument is given. A judgement about which side is right and why would finish this off well.

9.4 The falsification symposium

The **falsification** symposium refers to a series of articles written in the 1950s which included and responded to Antony Flew's initial presentation of falsification.

The scientific background

The philosopher Karl Popper (1902–1994) devised the falsification theory as a test for what is science and what is merely pseudo-science (a theory that is pretending to be scientific). Popper argues that when scientists make a claim, they invite others to test their hypothesis to see if it can be disproved. Whether I claim that water boils at 100 degrees or whether I claim that it turns into jam at −10 degrees, either way those claims are testable and if they were false you could show them to be false.

Popper uses this to criticise Freud's psychology. Theories such as the Oedipus complex are not falsifiable. Popper's point is that if it cannot be subject to tests that would show how it could be false, then this is not a real scientific theory. It is just pseudo-science.

Flew and the garden

The philosopher Antony Flew (1923–2010) applied this principle to the use of religious language. The problem with religious language is that it cannot be falsified and it is this consideration that means that religious statements are not statements at all.

He illustrates this with a story adapted from John Wisdom of two explorers finding what seems to be a garden. One explorer believes that there is a gardener, the other does not. As they wait and watch, set up trip wires and use dogs to sniff out the gardener, no gardener is found. The 'believer' continues to argue that the gardener exists but the story has now changed: he must be an invisible, intangible gardener who works in secret.

> **Key quote**
>
> But what remains of your original assertion? Just how does what you call an invisible, intangible, eternally elusive gardener differ from an imaginary gardener or even from no gardener at all?
>
> Antony Flew

Flew's conclusions about religious language

- Religious claims about the world aren't really claims at all as they cannot be tested.
- When challenged, the believer waters down their claim. They shift the goalposts so much that they are not saying anything at all. Flew states that religious claims suffer 'the death of a thousand qualifications'.

To illustrate this, consider the problem of evil. When a believer is challenged over their claim that 'God loves people' it reduces to 'God loves people but allows free will, develops character, does not intervene, has a bigger plan, and moves in mysterious ways'. Flew would ask how this would differ from there being no God at all. What would have to happen in order for God to be disproved?

Now test yourself

TESTED

4 Flew argues that religious statements are not _____.

> **Key word**
>
> **Falsification** The principle that a statement is a genuine scientific assertion if it is possible to say how it could be disproved empirically

> **Typical mistake**
>
> Some candidates write that Flew has shown religious language to be meaningless. While this is not completely wrong, it is inaccurate in terms of what Flew himself says. His point is that religious statements are not 'genuine assertions'.

9.5 Assessing the views presented in the falsification symposium

Flew's article set down a challenge to religious language. Two thinkers, Hare and Mitchell, respond to this challenge. Like Flew they also use parables.

> **Key word**
>
> **Blik** A basic unfalsifiable belief

R.M. Hare (1919–2002)

Parable	Hare's point	Discussion
A lunatic is convinced that all the dons (professors) at the university want to kill him. His friends arrange for him to meet the kindest dons they can find. However, this does not convince him; the lunatic replies that this just shows how cunning the dons are; they are trying to lull him into a false sense of security.	Hare is trying to defend religious belief on the grounds that Flew misunderstands the language involved. Flew is wrong to apply scientific criteria to theological language. Hare argues that we all have basic beliefs that he calls 'bliks'. Some bliks are reasonable but others are not. Religious belief is a blik and as such it cannot be empirically tested.	Hare is influenced by Wittgenstein's language games (see page 79). If Hare is right that religious belief is not scientific, then this allows religious statements to have meaning to the individual; the challenge Flew makes fails. This may seem inadequate as believers claiming that 'God loves us' are not just claiming a subjective truth; they believe themselves to be making a claim about reality as a whole.

Basil Mitchell (1917–2011)

Parable	Mitchell's point	Discussion
In a war-torn country, a partisan (resistance fighter) meets a stranger who persuades him that he is the secret commander of the resistance despite sometimes working undercover. Afterwards the stranger sometimes helps, but is also often seen in the uniform of the opposition handing over resistance fighters. When challenged, the partisan says, 'The stranger knows best.'	Mitchell partly accepts Flew's point. He suggests that there is evidence that counts for and against belief: the believer recognises that the problem of evil is a problem. However, the believer does not allow the evidence to decisively count against belief. This is because he/she is not a detached observer but is committed by faith to trust in God.	Mitchell recognises the role of evidence in a way that Hare does not. If the believer is like Hare's lunatic, then evidence is irrelevant. Mitchell rejects the idea that religious beliefs are bliks. Mitchell supports Flew's idea that religious statements are assertions or claims but, unlike Flew, sees a genuine role for faith.

Other views on falsification

- John Hick (see the Parable of the road, page 76) prefers verification to falsification as a test of religious statements. He notes that the two ideas, verification and falsification, are not opposites. If religious belief is true, it can be verified eschatologically, yet if it is false it cannot be shown to be false. Hence verification is a better test.
- Richard Swinburne has also questioned whether verification or falsification is the correct test for religious statements. He uses an illustration of toys in the cupboard coming alive at night when no one is watching them. Although it is an unverifiable and unfalsifiable statement, it is meaningful as we can understand the claim it makes. However, critics accuse Swinburne of oversimplifying the issue.

5 What is meant by the term 'blik?'
6 Does Mitchell agree with Flew or Hare? (Careful!)

9.6 Wittgenstein and language games

Wittgenstein on language

Wittgenstein's approach to philosophy and language can best be seen in the three short quotes below:

'Philosophical problems arise when language goes on holiday.'

Many of the problems that philosophers have wrestled with have been caused by a failure to pay attention to language.

'What is your aim in philosophy? To show the fly the way out of the fly bottle.'

If philosophical problems are caused by a lack of attention to language – and this traps philosophers – then the aim of philosophy has to be to focus on language in order to solve these problems.

'Don't ask for the meaning, ask for the use.'

Wittgenstein notes that the meanings of words are not rigid and fixed. What is more important is how a word is used. The meaning of a word is really its use. This use of language helps to create our perspective of the world.

Language games and religious language

Wittgenstein argues that language use is like playing a game with rules. Within our groups, we have agreed rules about how words are used. If we were to point at a chair and say the word 'hamster' then the person we are speaking to would correct us just like someone would do if we moved a chess piece incorrectly.

Wittgenstein observes that religious language and the language of different religious groups is in itself a language game. If we were to say that 'God allows suffering to develop our character and we will be rewarded in heaven', we cannot say the statement is true in a literal sense but it fits with a Christian interpretation of the world. It is not a statement that fits within the atheistic or Hindu language games, for instance. To suggest that the best explanation of evil is that God does not exist would not fit within the rules of the game. It would be rather like a swimmer choosing to use a boat in an Olympic race. It is not within the rules of the game.

What is true?

Essentially Wittgenstein argues that for the religious statement, there is not a difference of opinion where one viewpoint is right and one is wrong, there are actually two different ways of seeing. One way of thinking about this is the famous duck–rabbit illustration. The person who claims it is a duck and the person who claims it is a rabbit see the illustration differently.

This leaves the question of the truth of religious language unresolved in terms of verifying or falsifying what is said. It also broadens the debate. Religious statements are meaningful to those within the group despite the fact that the statements are not cognitive.

Now test yourself

7 What does Wittgenstein mean by the phrase 'letting the fly out of the fly bottle'?

8 Wittgenstein believes that religious statements are meaningful/meaningless and are cognitive/non-cognitive. (Cross out the incorrect terms.)

9.7 Wittgenstein assessed

Assessing Wittgenstein's theory of language

Strengths of Wittgenstein's theory	Weaknesses of Wittgenstein's theory
• Wittgenstein recognises that religious and scientific statements are two different types of things that deserve to be treated differently. • The theory recognises that meaning is not fixed but changes with use and context. • It recognises that there are beliefs that we have that are groundless. We cannot necessarily provide reasons for them yet they shape our world.	• A believer may reject the idea that religious statements only have meaning to the individual; they may (like Flew and Mitchell argue) see them as truth claims. They believe themselves to be making cognitive statements. • It has been argued that language games are circular. The language game gives words their meaning, yet the game itself is just a collection of words. • Critics claim Wittgenstein over-analyses language. He 'takes apart a perfectly working clock and then wonders why it doesn't work' (Gellner).

Comparing the ideas of Aquinas and Wittgenstein

Key area 1. Does a cognitive approach (such as Aquinas' thinking on analogy) or a non-cognitive approach (such as the language games concept of Wittgenstein) present a better way of making sense of religious language?

- Religious believers, such as Aquinas, understand themselves to be speaking cognitively about God.
- Ayer and Flew have challenged the cognitive view; Wittgenstein recognises that this is a challenge that has to be answered.
- Unlike Aquinas, Wittgenstein seems to suggest that only those 'within the game' are able to understand religious language.

Key area 2. How does a non-cognitive approach affect the interpretation of religious texts?

- A non-cognitive approach to scripture would suggest that 'Jesus rose from the dead' is not a historical claim but is a way of seeing and understanding the world. For some Christians, this type of approach is a step too far and weakens key elements of Christianity.
- Religious believers do interpret some texts symbolically. Few believe that the *Genesis* accounts of creation are literal truths. For some, the key to religious texts is not their literal truth but their function within faith communities. Wittgenstein may well have supported such a view.
- Aquinas' own view of scripture is very different to scholars who take a critical view of Biblical texts. Aquinas sees texts cognitively; they make claims that are true in reality.

Key area 3. How far does Aquinas' analogical view of theological language remain valuable in philosophy of religion?

- On a practical level, Aquinas' approach is still used within Christianity and offers some insight into the nature of God without reducing God to a human level (see page 70).
- The discussion goes beyond language to some degree and perspectives on this question may be driven by beliefs about scripture and the relative importance of reason and revelation (see the Christianity section of the specification), e.g. to what extent does the world (and hence our language) reveal truths about God?

> **Exam tip**
>
> One way of assessing Wittgenstein might be to contrast his approach to language with that of the verificationists and falsificationists. They argue that religious statements are cognitive and thus meaningless. Wittgenstein argues that statements are meaningful but are non-cognitive.

> **Making links**
>
> In order to consider the contrast between Aquinas and Wittgenstein more fully, you will need to review Chapter 8.4 on Aquinas and analogy.

Now test yourself

TESTED

9 What are the key differences between Aquinas and Wittgenstein's views of language?

9.8 Summary and exam tips

Exam checklist

- Explain and assess the verification principle, including Ayer's approach to verification.
- Consider whether verificationism is successful in showing religious language to be meaningless.
- Explain and assess Wittgenstein's views of language games and forms of life.
- Compare Wittgenstein's views with the cognitive approach to language taken by Aquinas.
- Explain and assess the ideas presented by the various thinkers in the falsification symposium.
- Assess whether any of the thinkers on falsification make a convincing case about religious language.

Revision activity

Copy and complete the table below. When you think you have learned the material, practise covering the table and explaining the ideas in your own words out loud. This could be done alongside a friend. Being able to explain something to someone else is the ultimate test of understanding!

Thinker(s)	Story	Key point
Vienna Circle		
		Verification in principle – need to be able to say how it would be possible to verify the statement. This makes religious statements meaningless
Flew		
	The lunatic	
Mitchell		
	Toys in the cupboard	
Wittgenstein		

Sample work

One of the key skills you will need if you are to gain good marks for AO2 is the ability to evaluate and discuss ideas. This is very different from asserting views. To say that a thinker has criticised a position is an *assertion*. To discuss whether that criticism is successful is *evaluation*. The following example from an essay discussing falsification illustrates the difference.

Basic answer	Better answer
Flew's views on falsification are rejected by R.M Hare. Hare gives the example of a lunatic who believes the dons at the university are trying to kill him. No matter what happens he refuses to give up this belief. Hare says that such beliefs are bliks. They cannot be falsified. Religious beliefs are bliks. This is a different understanding of what religious statements are.	Flew's views on falsification are rejected by R.M Hare. Hare gives the example of a lunatic who believes the dons at the university are trying to kill him. No matter what happens he refuses to give up this belief. Hare says that such beliefs are bliks. They cannot be falsified. Hare observes two key issues with Flew's view of language. Flew is mistaken in treating religious and scientific statements in the same way and, unlike scientific claims, believers care deeply about the claims they make. This second point seems to create a problem for Hare. Unlike the falsificationist, Hare's religious believer is unable to look at the evidence objectively, as illustrated by Hare's parable of the lunatic. However, it may just be that Hare is reflecting something of our human nature; we are, for better or for worse, trapped in our own worldviews.

Glossary

A posteriori Knowledge which is dependent on sense experience, can only be known after sense experience

A posteriori reasoning Reasoning that uses observation or experience to reach conclusions

A priori Knowledge which is not dependent on experience, can be known 'prior' to experience, e.g. triangles have three sides

A priori reasoning Reasoning that uses analytical deduction

Agnosticism The idea that God's nature and existence cannot be known

Analogy A comparison between two things in order to help us understand the less familiar thing

Anthropomorphic The tendency to describe something in human terms

Apophatic way (via negativa) The idea that the only way of speaking about God and religious ideas is through negative terms, what God is not

Arbitrary Random

Attribute A quality or descriptor

Benevolent Disposed towards kindliness; of God, used of love and compassion

Blik A basic unfalsifiable belief

Cataphatic way (via positiva) The idea that God can be spoken of in positive terms

Category mistake A problem in philosophy where something is thought and talked about in the wrong way; it belongs to a different category of thing

Cognitive Statements about God that can be known to be either true or false

Contingent being Something that relies on something else for its existence; it is possible that it does or does not exist

Conversion An experience which causes a sudden or gradual change in someone's belief system

Corporate experience An experience that is shared by a group

Covenant A legal-type agreement with consequences for being obeyed or disobeyed; in the Bible, the general idea that God will look after his people if they will follow him appropriately

Deism The idea that God causes or creates the world but is then separate and uninvolved

Determining predicate A description that adds something to the understanding about the subject

Efficient cause What brought something about or what made it

Empiricism The idea that observations via our senses lead us to understanding of the world

Epistemic distance The gap in knowledge between God and humanity; human inability to know God fully

Epistemology The branch of philosophy concerned with the theory of knowledge

Equivocal The idea that the same word is used with two completely different meanings

Eternal Separate to time; timeless

Everlasting Within the timeline; from beginning to end

Fall The moment when Adam and Eve disobeyed God by eating the fruit of the forbidden tree; humans are 'fallen' because of this moment

Falsification The principle that a statement is a genuine scientific assertion if it is possible to say how it could be disproved empirically

Final cause The purpose or reason for something

Formal cause What form or structure does something have, what is it that makes it that type of thing?

Forms The name Plato gives to ideal concepts that exist in reality

Immutable The idea that God does not change

Impassive The idea that God does not experience feelings or emotions

Inconsistent triad A triad (three things) of items that do not seem to be able all to be true at the same time – in this case, God being all-powerful, all-loving and evil existing

Ineffable Unable to be expressed or described in words, beyond description

Innocent suffering The suffering experienced by those who do not deserve it

Instrumental good A good that is good for a particular purpose

Leibniz law If two objects are identical they have to have exactly the same properties. So if object A and object B don't both have a certain property then they must be different

Logical fallacy An error in logic

Logical positivism A movement in philosophy that believed that the aim of philosophers should be to analyse language, particularly the language of science

Material cause What a substance is made of

Materialism The idea that human beings are made up of physical matter alone

Metaphysics The branch of philosophy dealing with the nature of reality, literally things 'beyond' or 'after' the physical realm

Moral evil Evil that is a result of human free choices

Mystical experience A direct experience of God or ultimate reality, a sense of oneness of all things

Natural evil Evil that comes from nature or natural sources

Necessary being Something that does not rely on anything else for its existence

Noetic Having the property of imparting knowledge

Non-cognitive Statements about God are not subject to truth or falsity

Numinous experience An experience of awe and wonder in the presence of an almighty God

Ockham's Razor The philosophical principle that 'you should not multiply entities beyond necessity'; that it is usually best to take the simplest explanation

Omnipotence All-powerful

Omniscience All-knowing

Ontological The study of being

Particulars The name Plato gives to the objects in the empirical world which are merely imperfect copies of the Form

Passivity The idea that the person having the religious experience is not taking the leading role; they are being 'acted upon'

Pluralism The idea in religion that truth is to be found in many faiths

Pragmatism A philosophical movement that argues that a theory must be treated as true if it works in practice

Privation A lack or absence of something

Rationalism The view that the primary source of knowledge is reason, in the strictest sense, a priori reason

Reason Using logical thought in order to reach conclusions

Soul-deciding theodicy A theodicy that emphasises that evil requires a decision from humans about whether they will follow God or give in to evil

Soul-making theodicy A theodicy that explains evil as a way of developing or making the soul

Substance dualism The idea that there are two aspects to human beings, the physical and the mental. The mental may be identified with the soul

Suffering Pain or harm experienced by a person

Tautology A phrase where the same thing is said twice in different words, e.g. the three-sided triangle

Teleological To do with something's purpose or goal or end point

Telos Literally 'end' or 'purpose'. The idea that everything has a purpose or aim

Theism The idea that God both creates and continues to be involved in the world

Theodicy A theory to justify God's righteousness (when faced with evil)

Transient An event that passes with time, temporary

Universal salvation The idea that everyone goes to heaven

Univocal The idea that words have the same meaning at all times

Verification principle The belief that statements are only meaningful if they can be verified by the senses. There are strong and weak forms of the principle generally associated with the Vienna Circle and A.J. Ayer, respectively

Now test yourself – answers

Chapter 1 Ancient philosophical influences

1 The real world, the world of the Forms, which lies beyond our world.
2 The philosophers should rule because they have knowledge, whereas the ordinary person does not.
3 The Form of the Good.
4 The final cause. It shows that Aristotle believes all things have purpose or *telos*.
5 Contrary to religious ideas of God, the Prime Mover is not omniscient and does not interact with or love the creation. It is a cause rather than a creator.
6 Existentialists believe that humans have to create their own purposes, whereas Aristotle believes that purpose is built into the structure of the universe.
7 Plato believes in a priori knowledge.
8 Aristotle believes in a posteriori knowledge.

Chapter 2 Soul, mind and body

1 Dualism believes that there are two parts or aspects to human beings – mind/soul and the body; materialism believes there is just one aspect, physical matter.
2 The soul is the real person: it is eternal, unchanging, non-physical and possesses knowledge. The body is not the real person; its physical needs are a nuisance. It is temporal, it changes, it is physical and only possesses opinions.
3 Plato understands the Form as something that exists beyond this world and as being more important than this world. For Aristotle, Form is the shape of individual objects within this world.
4 The argument from doubt and the argument from divisibility.
5 The Cogito is short for *cogito ergo sum* ('I think, therefore I am') – Descartes' proof of his own existence. Whilst thought is occurring there must be a thinker.
6 Dawkins believes that the soul was merely an ancient attempt to understand consciousness. It is now an unnecessary idea as science provides a better explanation.
7 The problem is that the mental and the physical seem to be incompatible substances and it is hard to see how they could interact in one person. It is like asking, 'How does the ghost ride the bicycle?'
8 A category mistake is where we make the mistake of treating one thing as if it were another type of thing. Ryle suggests that dualists are thinking of the mind in the wrong way. It is not an extra thing. He illustrates this with his example of the visitor to the university.

Chapter 3 Arguments based on observation

1 Reasoning based on the use of evidence or experience.
2 Aristotle.
3 Arrow, archer.
4 A rock or stone.
5 It still shows evidence of being designed, even if it is broken when it is seen.
6 Motion (or change), causation (or cause and effect), contingency and necessity.
7 This being is what we call God.
8 A shipbuilder does not usually work alone; he is also likely to have learned his trade through a process of trial and error; and just because he creates a great ship, it does not mean that he is a moral person in himself.
9 Natural selection.
10 An error in logic – bad thinking.

Chapter 4 Arguments based on reason

1 Reasoning based on analysis or logic.
2 The study of being.
3 That than which nothing greater can be conceived (or thought of) – the greatest possible being.
4 Existing in both the mind and reality.
5 God is a special case, a necessary being, unlike Gaunilo's island.
6 The existence of the subject of the sentence.
7 Thaler.
8 God.
9 Antony Flew.

Chapter 5 Religious experience

1 It should be judged by its effects, the 'fruit' it produces.
2 They are ineffable, noetic, transient and passive.
3 It is an experience where there is a sudden or gradual change in someone's belief system.
4 Starbuck shows that conversion experiences are similar to normal non-religious experiences where adolescents go through a process of finding their identity.
5 The principle of testimony is Swinburne's suggestion that we should give people the benefit of the doubt and believe their claims to religious experience unless there is a good reason not to. This can be criticised as religious experiences are very different to everyday experiences and we may have reason to question the reliability of individuals involved.
6 Freud, along with Feuerbach, suggests that desire for religious experience is based on wishful thinking and that the experiences themselves are triggered by our subconscious.
7 The God helmet produces a magnetic field which causes something akin to a religious experience in many people's brains. Some scientists have used this to argue that religious experiences are entirely natural and hence are nothing to do with God.
8 A corporate religious experience is a religious experience that is shared by a group of people. The events at Fatima, Medjugorje and the Toronto Blessing are examples of such experiences.

Chapter 6 The problem of evil

1 Natural: tornadoes, tsunamis, poverty, pollution. Moral: theft, genocide. For some of these natural evils, consider if they can have been caused by moral evil: pollution by human activity, poverty by corrupt governments and so on.
2 An attempt to justify the righteousness of God in the face of evil and suffering.
3 Logically it seems that God cannot be all-powerful and all-loving if evil also exists – the three do not seem to be able to go together logically.
4 A lack of something – Augustine says that evil is a lack of good, rather than a substance in itself.
5 Harmony was lost at the Fall and the disharmony in the world has led to natural evil.
6 Augustine's theodicy describes the process of humans making choices (deciding) to move away from the punishment for sin.
7 God's likeness.

8 The world is a place where the conditions are such that we can 'make' our souls into better souls – the likeness of God. Suffering is one such condition.
9 Jesus on the cross.

Chapter 7 The nature or attributes of God

1 Descartes.
2 Aquinas and Swinburne.
3 The idea that omnipotent means almighty: self-imposed limitation.
4 The nature of the knower.
5 Space (three dimensions: length, breadth and height) and time.
6 It fits with the portrayal of God in the Bible.
7 (a) Geach; (b) Schleiermacher.
8 Simple and conditional.
9 Anselm.
10 *hesed.*
11 Either God defines goodness – everything God does is good by definition – or else God is subject to an independent standard of goodness.

Chapter 8 Religious language

1 This is where words have the same meaning in two different contexts.
2 This is where words have a different meaning in different contexts.
3 They argue that God is beyond description. Words are inadequate to describe him. The only way of speaking correctly and respectfully of God is by describing what he is not.
4 Analogy of attribution.
5 Proportion.
6 It is not univocal so does not reduce God to our level (avoids anthropomorphism), but is not equivocal so does allow some statements about God (avoids agnosticism).
7 A sign points at something, whereas a symbol participates in that to which it points.
8 Art, like symbolic language, communicates on a deep emotional level.

Chapter 9 Twentieth-century perspectives

1 Cognitive statements are statements that are able to be true or false. Non-cognitive statements are statements that are not subject to truth and falsity.
2 Ayer gives a broader criterion in suggesting that statements are meaningful if there is a way to

verify them in principle, whereas the Vienna Circle suggested that statements need verifying directly in order to be meaningful.

3 Eschatological verification is Hick's idea that religious statements are verifiable after death, and thus are meaningful.

4 Genuine assertions.

5 This is Hare's term for a basic unfalsifiable belief.

6 Mitchell partly agrees with both thinkers. He agrees with Flew that religious statements are subject to some empirical testing. He also accepts Hare's point that religious believers have a faith commitment that may mean beliefs cannot be falsified.

7 Philosophers cause themselves unnecessary problems by failing to pay attention to language. The aim of philosophy is to focus on language in order to avoid these problems.

8 Wittgenstein believes that religious statements are meaningful and are cognitive.

9 Aquinas has a cognitive view of language, whereas Wittgenstein has a non-cognitive view. Aquinas believes religious concepts have an objective meaning, whereas Wittgenstein believes meaning is relative to the group using the statement.